GRANDPA SAYS THE WOLD MUST HELP TIBETANS LIBERATE TIBET

COL (RETD) BHASKAR SARKAR VSM

This book is dedicated to the six million simple, peaceful, charming, Buddhist people of Tibet, who are subjected to unspeakable violations of their human rights under Chinese rule.

Contents

Acknowledgements

I am grateful to Ms Sarita Sharma for designing the front cover.

Prologue

The so-called free world, the US, EU, UK, Canada, India, Australia, pay lip service to colonization of Tibet and Xinjian and human rights abuses by China in its colonies. They need to do more for the unfortunate people of these regions. **They need to severely sanction China and support the struggle for independence of these people. This book is on helping Tibetans liberate of Tibet.**

The free world led by the UN, US, EU, India, Canada, Australia and Japan are great at talking about human rights and imposing economic sanctions on a few. They happily pay lip service to the abuse of human rights in Israel and Palestine, in Afghanistan, Tibet, Xinjiang, Myanmar and many other places. **It is time the free world helped the freedom fighters of these countries fight their colonizers and their tormentors with money, arms, training and intelligence. It is time the free world to help the Tibetan people regain their freedom.**

India is the only country in the free world which has common borders with Tibet. It is also the most affected by Chinese presence in Tibet. **It can and must help Tibetans fight for their freedom and preserve their rich cultural heritage.**

When Pakistan was committing genocide in East Pakistan in 1970 and a million refugees came to India, Mrs Indira Gandhi went round the free world seeking action against Pakistan. Not one country of the free world lifted a little finger to protect the human rights of the Bengalis. President Nixon even sent the Seventh Fleet to save Pakistan. Only Russia helped India help liberate Bangladesh. Our beloved Prime Minister, Modiji, is immensely popular and influential among world leaders. Grandpa is sure that he will fare better than Mrs Gandhi and get the Free World help Tibetans free themselves from Chinese rule.

Mrs. Indira Gandhi helped Bengalis of East Bengal create the Mukti Bahini to fight and liberate their country. She armed, trained, funded and provided leadership to the Mukti Bahini with volunteers from the Indian Army. She also provided Mukti Bahini bases in India and provided them artillery support when required from India territory. **Can our beloved Prime Minister do the same for the Tibetan Resistance?**

Our political leaders and administrators have a "see no evil mentality" and a pacifist mindset. Pandit Nehru was either so gullible or weak that he saw no danger in the induction of Chinese Army into Tibet or found it expedient to ignore it. There was no monitoring of Chinese activities in Aksai Chin area of Ladakh. Our government became aware of Chinese incursions only after the Chinese had annexed Aksai Chin. We paid no attention to modernizing our defence forces till after the 1962 debacle. We fought the state of art American Patton tanks of the Pakistan Army during 1965 War with Second World War Sherman and Centurion tanks. We allowed Pakistan to quietly occupy Kargil. The present Government is not very different. One hears "War is not an option." Our leaders like Lal Bahadur Shastri, Indira Gandhi and Atal Behari Vajpayee never said that. Neither did General Kariappa, General Choudhury or General Manekshaw say so. Ukraine is ready to take on might Russia. Taiwan is ready to take on China. We, call ourselves the greatest, but are reluctant to take on China.

We tolerate China's unfriendly acts, their arming of Pakistan with nuclear and modern weapon systems, their support for Pakistan's support for terrorists in Kashmir at the UN and other international forums, their support for terrorist operating in the North East like the Naga Underground, ULFA etc that has continued unabated since the 1950s. We look aside when China gets our neighbours, Nepal, Myanmar, Bangladesh, Sri Lanka into debt traps and force them to allow anti Indian activities. We did not tolerate Pakistani genocide of the Bengalis of East Pakistan. But we tolerate the genocide of Tibetans and Uighurs, the crushing of democracy in Myanmar and do not raise our little finger to help them. Was Indira Gandhi the difference?

India needs to help Tibetans liberate Tibet and secure our northern borders. In this venture, India must seek the help of the free world. It must be ready to go ahead, even if the other countries turn their back. We have the most to gain.

It is not out of place to mention that all information connected to military strengths of countries, economic data etc are based either the Internet and published books. No access to classified information has been has been made.

This is my sixth book in the Grandpa series. The other five are "Grandpa's Selection – Outstanding Victories of the Indian Army"; "Grandpa's Tales – Ambush and Other Stories"; "Grandpa's Tips on Management for All", "Grandpa's Tips on Navigating Through Life" and "Grandpa's Tips on Keeping Fit with Homeopathy, Allopathy, Traditional

Medicines and Self-medication". All the books are available on Amazon, Flipkart and notionpress.com.

Col (Retd) Bhaskar Sarkar VSM

colbhaskarvsm@gmail.com

Contents

CHAPTER ONE

History of Tibet

Very little is known about Grandpa about the history of Tibet till 6th Century. The first dynasty in the records is the Yarlung Dynasty. It was established by Nyatri Tsenpo around 126 BC in the valley of the Yarlung River about 90 km south east of present day Lasha. The Dynasty prospered and grew in size. By 630 AD, it grew into the Tibetan Empire under the rule of Namri Songsten. The first known interaction between China and Tibet was in 640, when the **Tibetan King Songtsen Gampo married the niece of the Tang Emperor Taizong. Gampo's descendants conquered the vast region that now forms the Chinese provinces of Qinghai, Gansu and Xinjiang (often referred to as inner Tibet) between 663 and 692. Namri Songsten is supposed to have sent two ambassadors to China in 608. Songsten Gampo was the first great emperor who extended Tibet's power beyond the Yarlung Valley.** Buddhism entered Tibet during his time. In 692, the Chinese retook Inner Tibet. The Tibetan king then allied himself with the Arabs and eastern Turks. Chinese Imperial forces under General Gao Xianzhi conquered Tibet and much of Central Asia, until he was defeated by the Arabs and Turks at the battle of Talas River in 751. The Chinese withdrew and Tibet regained control of much of Xinjiang and Inner Tibet. Tibetans even seized the Tang Chinese capital city of Changan (now Xian) in 763. **Tibet and China signed a peace treaty in 821 or 822, which delineated the border between the two empires.** Status quo was maintained till the rise of the Mongols under Genghis Khan who conquered China and Tibet. By the 9th Century, the Tibetan Empire had extended up to the Pala Kingdom of Bengal in India to the south and Mongolia to the North. The Pala emperor, Dharam Pala, is reported to have accepted Tibetan suzerainty.

Tibetan Kingdom in Ladakh

Upon the death of Langdarma, the last of the Yarlung Dynasty, a succession struggle resulted in the breakup of the empire. **In 930, Nimya-Gon, one of the warlords of Tibet, established the first Ladakh Dynasty. His kingdom extended from Mayum La in the east to Zojila in the west.** After his death, the vast kingdom was divided into three. The eldest, Lachen Palgyion got Ladakh (Zojila to Demchok), the second son Trashigong got Guge Kingdom which included Ngari, Rutog and Purang (region at trijunction of Tibet, Nepal and Uttarakhand) regions in western Tibet as also Upper Kinnaur and Spiti and the third son got Zanskar or the land between Kashmir and Ladakh including Kargil. The capital of the Guge kingdom was at Tsaparang in the Sutlej valley near Mount Kailash. **This is perhaps the basis of Chinese claim of the territory of Ladakh and certain tracts of Kinnaur and Spiti.**

Ladakh came under the Ladakhi Namgyal Dynasty in 1460. It was established by Lhachen Bhagan in alliance with the people of Leh by defeating the Tibetan king. The Dynasty remained in power till 1842 when the Dogra General Zorawar Singh conquered Ladakh. Sengee Namgyal (the Lion King) carried out a lot of development work including building the Leh Palace. Namgyal kings attacked Guge Kingdom and conquered its capital Tsaparang in 1682. This led to the rulers of Guge to seek help of the Central Tibetan Government under the 5th Dalai Lama. Tibetan forces then attacked Ladakh. The King of Ladakh was forced to seek the help of the Mughals to save his kingdom. Stalemate was reached in 1684. **The war ended with the Treaty of Tingmosang which laid down the agreed boundaries between Ladakh and Tibet.** Guge, Purang and Rutog became part of Tibet with the western border with Ladakh being fixed along Lah-ri stream near Demchok. Tsaparang and the Guge kingdom became a part of the Lhasa-based Central Tibetan government under the leadership of the 5th Dalai Lama.

Mongol Tibet

Returning to Tibet, the region came to be dominated by the Sakya lama, who established the Sakya Dynasty with the help of the Mongols. The Mongols invaded Tibet in 1240 but withdrew their soldiers 1241, as all the Mongol princes were called back to Mongolia in preparation for the appointment of a successor to Ogedei Khan. **They returned to the region in 1244. They annexed Amdo and Kham regions in eastern Tibet and appointed Tibetan Lama Sakya Paṇḍita as the Viceroy of Central Tibet 1249. Thus, Tibet was incorporated into the Mongol Empire. Tibetans however were allowed to follow their religious practices and run local**

affairs. The Mongols retained nominal power over religious and regional political affairs. Tibetan Lama Chogyal Phagpa took over as Viceroy in 1265. **The Mongols under Kublai Khan defeated the Southern Song Empire in the Battle of Yamen in 1271 and established the first non-Han Yuan Dynasty in China. Tibet came to be considered one of the thirteen provinces of Mongol Yuan Empire.** The Kingdoms of Guge in Western Tibet retained its internal autonomy.

Tibet Gains De Facto Independence

The Sakya Dynasty continued to rule Tibet as a part of the Yuan Empire. **In 1351, the Mongolian Yuan Dynasty was defeated by the Han Song Dynasty.** Tibet reasserted its independence and refused to pay tribute to the new Emperor. The Sakya Dynasty ended in 1358 when Central Tibet including Lasha was taken over by Marpa Kotsaya of the Kagyu sect. The next 80 years were a period of relative instability. The Mongols' Yuan Empire fell in 1368 to the Han Chinese Ming Dynasty. In Tibet, various warlords vied for power. **In 1474, the Lama of an important Tibetan Buddhist monastery, Gendun Drup, passed away. A child, Gendun Gyatso, who born two years later was found to be a reincarnation of the Lama and was raised to be the next leader of that sect. After their lifetimes, the two men were called the First and Second Dalai Lama.** Their sect, the Gelug or "Yellow Hats," became the dominating sect of Tibetan Buddhism. **The Third Dalai Lama, Sonam Gyatso (1543-1588) was responsible for converting the Mongols to Gelug Tibetan Buddhism.** The Mongol ruler Altan Khan was a follower of the Dalai Lama. The Gtsang-pa Dynasty assumed the royal throne of Tibet in 1562 and ruled Tibet for the next 80 years. **The Fourth Dalai Lama, Yonten Gyatso (1589-1616), was a Mongolian prince and the grandson of Altan Khan.** The Gtsang-Pa Dynasty was overthrown by the Tsangpa Dynasty of Shighaste in 1565. They played a major role in bringing Dalai Lamas to power in 1640.

Tibet Under Chinese Qing Dynasty

During the 1630s, China was embroiled in power struggles between Mongols, Han Chinese of the fading Ming Dynasty and the Manchu people of north-eastern China (Manchuria) and were unable to dominate Tibet. **The Manchus eventually defeated the Han in 1644 and establish China's last imperial dynasty, the Qing Dynasty (1644-1912).**

Tibet saw a power struggle between Kagyu (Red Hats) Tibetan Buddhists and the Yellow Hats in 1634. The great general Gushi Khan, of the Oirad Mongols supported the Yellow Hats who prevailed. **The Fifth**

Dalai Lama, Lobsang Gyatso, became the spiritual and temporal Head over all of Tibet in 1642 with Mongol help.The Potala Palace in Lhasa was constructed as a symbol of this new synthesis of secular and temporal power. The Dalai Lama made a state visit to the Qing Dynasty's second Emperor, Shunzhi, in 1653. The Dalai Lama was recognized as the spiritual authority of the Qing Empire. The fifth Dalai Lama died in 1682. This was followed by a succession struggle. The Sixth Dalai Lama was finally enthroned in 1697. His unconventional lifestyle prompted Lobsang Khan of the Khoshud Mongols to depose him in 1705. Lobsang Khan seized control of Tibet, named himself King and appointed a pretender Dalai Lama. Lobsang Khan ruled for 12 years until the Dzungar Mongols invaded and took power. They killed the pretender to the Dalai Lama's throne. This was appreciated by the Tibetan people. But the Mongols then began to loot monasteries around Lhasa. This vandalism brought a quick response from the Qing Emperor Kangxi, who sent Chinese troops into Tibet. The Dzungars defeated the Imperial Chinese army near Lhasa in 1718. In 1720, Emperor Kangxi sent another, larger force to Tibet, which crushed the Dzungars. **The Qing army also brought the proper Seventh Dalai Lama, Kelzang Gyatso (1708-1757) to Lhasa and installed him as the ruler of Tibet.** China took advantage of this period of instability in Tibet to seize the regions of Amdo and Kham, including them into the Chinese province of Qinghai in 1724. However, the area was ruled through Tibetan nobles. Three years later, the Chinese and Tibetans signed a treaty that laid out the boundary line between the two nations which remained in force until 1910.

The Dzungar Khanate, a Mongol Empire, invaded Tibet in 1717. They deposed the acting Dalai Lama and also defeated a small combined force of Tibetan and Chinese forces sent by Qing empire. in 1718. In response, a larger force was sent by the Chinese Emperor. This force together with Tibetan forces under the governor of Western Tibet expelled the Dzungars from Tibet in 1720. The Qing Emperor installed a new, more popular Dalai Lama, Kelzang Gyatso as the 7th Dalai Lama and left behind a garrison of 3,000 men in Lhasa. Qing Emperors thus became overlords of Tibet and Tibet was turned into a protectorate. **In 1721, the Qing Emperor removed the indigenous civil government that had existed in Lhasa since the rule of the 5th Dalai Lama and created a Tibetan cabinet or council of ministers known as the Kashag.This council governed Tibet under the close supervision of the Chinese garrison commander stationed in Lhasa. Dalai Lama's role became more symbolic. Thus began the period of Qing**

Dynasty administrative rule of Tibet which lasted until the fall of the Qing empire in 1912. More than 1300 Chinese soldiers were stationed by the Qing Empire in Tibet to support the 3,000 strong Tibetan army.

The Dalai Lama was sent to Lithang Monastery in Kham. The Panchen Lama was brought to Lhasa and was given temporal authority over Tsang and Ngari, creating a territorial division between the two high lamas that was to be a long-lasting feature of Chinese policy toward Tibet. The Dalai Lama returned to Lhasa in 1735, temporal power remained with the Panchen Lama. The Qing found the Panchen Lama to be a loyal agent and an effective ruler over a stable Tibet, so he remained dominant until his death in 1747. **The Qing Emperor re-organized the Tibetan government again 1747 and restored temporal power to the Dalai Lama.** The Dalai and Panchen Lamas were no longer allowed to petition the Qing Emperor directly but could only do so through Ambans or Chinese regents.

In 1788, the Regent of Nepal sent a Gurkha army to invade Tibet. The Qing Emperor responded in strength and the Nepalese retreated. The Gurkhas returned three years later, plundering and destroying some famous Tibetan monasteries. The Chinese sent a force of 17,000 which, along with Tibetan troops, drove the Gurkhas out of Tibet to within 30 km of Kathmandu. Despite this sort of assistance from the Chinese Empire, the people of Tibet chafed under increasingly meddlesome Qing rule. Between 1804, when the Eighth Dalai Lama died, and 1895, when the Thirteenth Dalai Lama assumed the throne, none of the incumbent incarnations of the Dalai Lama lived to see their nineteenth birthdays. If the Chinese found a certain incarnation too hard to control, they would poison him. If the Tibetans thought an incarnation was controlled by the Chinese, then they would poison him themselves.

In 1841, the Sikh kingdom of Jammu and Kashmir attempted to establish their authority on Western Tibet. **This led to the Sino-Sikh War (1841–1842). Forces under General Zorawar Singh conquered much of Western Tibet. The Qing Emperors sent reinforcements. Winter and lack of cooperation by British India weakened the Jammu and Kashmir Army which was defeated at the Battle of Minsar. General Zorawar Singh was killed. The Chinese now attacked Ladakh and laid siege on Leh. The Jammu and Kashmir Kingdom sent reinforcement. The Tibetan forces were defeated at the Battle of Chusul in 1842. In the peace treaty that followed, the Chinese accepted Ladakh to be a part of the Sikh Empire. The Sikh Empire gave up claims to western Tibet. Both sides agreed** to respect "earlier traditional borders". The British defeated the Sikhs in 1846. This resulted in transfer of sovereignty over Ladakh to the British. However, both the British and Tibetans were apparently sufficiently satisfied that a traditional border was recognized and defined by natural elements and the border was not demarcated. **Since these borders are not clearly defined, there is an ongoing border dispute between China and India.**

Alarmed by the Dalai Lama's assertive attitude, the Qing Government appointed Zhao Erfan, the Governor of Qinghai province in western China bordering Tibet, "Army Commander of Tibet" to reintegrate Tibet into China. He was sent in 1905 on a punitive mission. His troops destroyed a number of monasteries in Kham and Amdo regions of Tibet. A process of imposing Han culture in the region was started. The Dalai Lama fled to India in 1906 and was once again deposed by the Chinese. **The Qing dynasty collapsed in October 1911,** Zhao's soldiers mutinied and beheaded him. All remaining Qing forces left Tibet.

British Invasion of Tibet

In 1903–04, a British expedition led by Colonel Younghusband was sent to Lhasa to force a trading agreement and to prevent Tibetans from establishing a relationship with the Russians. The 13th Dalai Lama fled to Outer Mongolia before the British arrived. He then went to Qing capital Beijing in 1908. The Anglo-Tibetan Treaty of Lhasa of 1904 was followed by the Sino-British Treaty of 1906. Beijing agreed to pay London 2.5 million rupees which Lhasa was forced to agree upon in the Anglo-Tibetan treaty of 1904. **In 1907, Britain and Russia accepted the suzerainty of China over Tibet.**

The Shimla Convention, a convention to negotiate the boundaries between Tibet, British India and China was held in Shimla in 1913-14. It provided that Western, Central and western Kham regions of Tibet would remain in the hands of the Tibetan Government in Lasha under Chinese suzerainty but China would not interfere in its administration. Amdo and eastern Kham regions will be administered by the Chinese Government. The boundary between Tibet and India would be the McMohan Line, and the Tibetan territory south of the McMohan Line, (Arunachal Pradesh) was ceded to the British. The draft was initialled by all three countries on 27 April 1914, but China immediately repudiated it. A slightly revised convention was signed again on 3 July 1914, but only by Britain and Tibet. The Chinese declined to sign it. The British and

Tibetan representatives then signed a bilateral declaration that stated that the convention would be binding on themselves. This convention is the basis of Chinese claim on Arunachal Pradesh.

Tibet Regains De Facto Independence

By 1911, China was in turmoil and unable to intervene in Tibet. Japan invaded Manchuria in 1910 and occupied most of Chinese coastal regions up to 1945. Second World War and finally another round of civil war followed. **The Tibetans took advantage of this turmoil and declared themselves independent in 1912. They enjoyed this independence till 1949.** The new government of the Republic of China held nominal power over the majority of Chinese territory for only four years before war broke out between numerous armed factions. China saw near continuous civil war up to the Communist victory in 1949

In 1912, China's new revolutionary government issued a formal apology to the Dalai Lama for the Qing Dynasty's insults and offered to reinstate him as the spiritual leader. The Dalai Lama refused. He then issued a proclamation that was distributed across Tibet, rejecting Chinese control and stating that "We are a small, religious and independent nation." The Dalai Lama took control of Tibet's internal and external governance in 1913. He negotiated directly with foreign powers and reformed Tibet's judicial, penal and educational systems. The 13th Dalai Lama ruled independent Tibet in peace until his death in 1933. Following his death, the new reincarnation of the Dalai Lama was born in Amdo in 1935. Tenzin Gyatso, the 14th and current Dalai Lama, was taken to Lhasa in 1937 to begin training for his duties as the leader of Tibet. He remained there until 1959 when he fled to India.

The Dalai Lama returned to Tibet from India in July 1912 after the fall of the Qing Dynasty. He expelled the Chinese regent and all Chinese troops. In 1913, the Dalai Lama proclaimed that Tibet a small, religious and independent nation. The Chinese government in the 1930s maintained that Tibet was a part of China. **The USA also recognised Tibet as a province of China in 1944.** Tibet continued to have very limited contacts with the rest of the world. British representatives were stationed in Gyantse, Yatung and Gartok (western Tibet) after the Younghusband Mission. These so-called "Trade Agents" became diplomatic representatives of the British Government of India and in 1936–37 the British also established a permanent mission in Lhasa. After India became independent in1947, the British mission was transferred to Indian government control.

Communist China and Tibet

The People's Republic of China (PRC), founded in October 1949 by the victorious Communists under the leadership of Mao Zedong lost no time in asserting Chinese hegemony in Tibet. **In October 1950, the People's Liberation Army (PLA) entered the Tibet at Chamdo.** In 1951, Tibetan representatives negotiated status of Tibet with the Chinese government. This resulted in a Seventeen Point Agreement which formalized China's sovereignty over Tibet. **This agreement was rejected by the Tibetan government-in-exile.** From 1951 to 1959, traditional Tibetan society with its lords and manorial estates continued to function unchanged. The Dalai Lama's government was permitted to function as usual. However, twenty thousand Chinese soldiers were deployed in Central Tibet. The Chinese built highways that reached Lhasa. The road network was then extended to the Indian, Nepalese and Pakistani borders. **Communists tried to establish rural communes in Inner Tibet, as was happening in the whole of China. Landholdings of the monasteries and nobility were seized for redistribution to the peasants. The communist forces hoped to destroy the power base of the wealthy and the Lamas within Tibetan society.** They established secular schools and broke the educational monopoly of the monasteries. They constructed running water and electrical systems in Lhasa.

By 1956 there was unrest in eastern Kham and Amdo, where land reform had been implemented in full. These rebellions eventually spread into western Kham and U-Tsang. **In 1956–57, armed Tibetan guerrillas ambushed convoys of the Chinese PLA. These rebellions eventually spread into Outer Tibet. The uprising was led by the monks and continued till 1973. The uprising received extensive assistance from the U.S. Central Intelligence Agency (CIA) who provided funds and military training and established support camps in Nepal. Initially the rebels had considerable success with CIA support and aid. Some parts of southern Tibet fell into rebel control.** The poorly armed Tibetans used guerrilla tactics in an attempt to drive out the Chinese. The PLA responded by razing entire villages and monasteries to the ground. The Chinese even threatened to blow up the Potala Palace and kill the Dalai Lama, but this threat was not carried out. According to the Dalai Lama's government in exile, the bitter fighting left an estimated 86,000 Tibetans dead.

In 1959, China's military crackdown on rebels in Kham and Amdo led to the "Lasha Uprising". Full scale resistance spread throughout Tibet.

Fearing capture of the Dalai Lama, unarmed Tibetans surrounded his residence. **Tibetan troops were able to secure a route for the Dalai Lama to escape into India on March 17, 1959.** Actual fighting began on March 19 and lasted only two days before the Tibetan troops were defeated. Much of Lhasa lay in ruins by March 20, 1959. An estimated 800 artillery shells had pummelled Norbulingka. Three of Lhasa's largest monasteries were essentially levelled. The Chinese rounded up thousands of monks and executed many of them. Monasteries and temples all over Lhasa were ransacked. The remaining members of the Dalai Lama's bodyguard were publicly executed by firing squad. **By the time of the 1964 census, 300,000 Tibetans had gone "missing" in the previous five years, either secretly imprisoned, killed or in exile. In the days after the 1959 Uprising, the Chinese government revoked most aspects of Tibet's autonomy, and initiated resettlement and land distribution across the country.** Following the Lhasa uprising and the Dalai Lama's flight from Tibet in 1959, the government of India was politically pressured by Britain and US to accept the Tibetan refugees. The Tibetan resistance forces withdrew into areas bordering Nepal and continued operations. **In 1973, on the eve of US President Kissinger's overtures to China, American support to the rebels was withdrawn and the Nepalese government dismantled the Tibetan resistance bases in Nepal.**

There were several waves of Tibetan refugees who fled Tibet and this led to the creation of Tibetan diasporas in India, the United States, and Europe. The American Society for a Free Asia, a CIA-financed front, supported the Tibetan resistance. The Dalai Lama's eldest brother played an active role in that organization. **The Dalai Lama's second-eldest brother established an intelligence operation with the CIA as early as 1951. He later upgraded it into a CIA-trained guerrilla unit whose recruits parachuted back into Tibet. CIA support ended when President Nixon decided to normalise relations with China. Thus, Tibetan resistance to Chinese rule ended.**

In 1965, the area that had been under the control of the Dalai Lama's government was renamed the Tibet Autonomous Region (TAR). Autonomy provided that the head of government would be an ethnic Tibetan. Actual power in the TAR is held by the First Secretary of the Tibet Autonomous Regional Committee of the Chinese Communist Party, who has never been a Tibetan. Most of Tibet's more than 6,000 monasteries were destroyed between 1959 and 1961 by the Communist Party of China. **Disturbances flared up again in 2008.** Many ethnic Hans and Huis were attacked in the riot, their shops vandalized or burned. The Chinese government reacted swiftly, imposing curfews and strictly limiting access to Tibetan areas.

In 2005, Chinese Premier Wen Jiabao offered to hold talks with the 14th Dalai Lama on the Tibet issue, provided he dropped the demand for independence.The Dalai Lama said in an interview with the South China Morning Post "We are willing to be part of the People's Republic of China, to have it govern and guarantee to preserve our Tibetan culture, spirituality and our environment." He had already said he would accept Chinese sovereignty over Tibet but insisted on real autonomy over its religious and cultural life. The Tibetan government in exile called on the Chinese government to respond. The move was seen to be unpopular with some Tibetans in exile, particularly among the younger generation.

On March 10, 2008, Tibetans marked the 49th anniversary of the 1959 uprising by peacefully protesting for the release of imprisoned monks and nuns. Chinese police broke up the protest with tear gas and gunfire. The protests continued for several more days and finally turned into a riot. Furious Tibetans ransacked and burned the shops of Han Chinese immigrants in Lhasa and other cities. The official Chinese media claimed that 18 people were killed by the rioters. China immediately cut off access to Tibet for foreign media and tourists. **The unrest spread to neighbouring Qinghai (Inner Tibet), Gansu, and Sichuan Provinces. The Chinese government cracked down hard and mobilized about 50,000 troops. Reports indicate that the military killed between 80 and 140 people and arrested more than 2,300 Tibetans.** The unrest came at a sensitive time for China, which was gearing up for the 2008 Summer Olympics in Beijing. The situation in Tibet caused increased international scrutiny of Beijing's entire human rights record, leading some foreign leaders to boycott the Olympic Opening Ceremonies. The same year, the Chinese government launched a 570-million-yuan (81.43 million U.S. dollars) project to preserve 22 historical and cultural heritage sites in Tibet, including the Zhaxi Lhunbo Lamasery, the Jokhang, Ramogia, Sanyai and Samgya-Goutog monasteries.

Tibetans in Exile in India

The community of Tibetans in exile established in Dharamsala (Himachal Pradesh) and Karnataka, South India, has expanded since 1959. Tibetans have duplicated Tibetan monasteries in India and now house tens of thousands of monks. They have also created Tibetan schools, hospitals and established the Library of Tibetan Works and Archives, all aimed at continuing Tibetan tradition and culture. Tibetan festivals such as Lama dances, celebration of Losar, the Tibetan New Year, and the Monlam continue in exile. The plight of the Tibetan refugees garnered international attention when the Dalai Lama, spiritual and religious leader of the Tibetan government in exile, won the Nobel Peace Prize in 1989. The Dalai Lama was awarded the Nobel Prize on the basis of his unswerving commitment to peaceful protest against the Chinese occupation of Tibet. Among the most recent ceremonies and awards, he was given the Congressional Gold Medal by President Bush in 2007 and in 2006 he was one of only three people to ever receive an honorary Canadian citizenship. The Chinese consistently protests each official contact with the exiled Tibetan leader by western countries and their leaders.

China's central government, in a bid to dilute the Tibetan population, initiated a "Western China Development Program" in 1978. As many as 300,000 Han Chinese now live in Tibet, two thirds of them in Lhasa. The Tibetan population of Lhasa, in contrast, is only 100,000. Ethnic Chinese hold the vast majority of government posts. In an attempt to gain acceptance, Beijing allowed the 10th Panchen Lama, Tibetan Buddhism's second-in-command, to return to Tibet in 1989. He died five days later at the age of 50, allegedly of a massive heart attack. China has made every effort to maintain a strangle hold on Tibet. Strict censorship is maintained. But occasionally, news of agitations by Tibetans and reports of human rights violations reaches the outside world. One such incident was the deaths at Drapchi Prison in 1998 where Tibetan criminal and political detainees were brutalized for shouting anti-Chinese and pro Dalai Lama slogans during a flag raising ceremony. Five nuns, three monks and one male criminal were reportedly killed by the guards.

Nothing has changed for Tibetans in Tibet. The Dalai Lama remains in India. He was awarded the Nobel Prize on the basis of his unswerving commitment to peaceful protest against the Chinese occupation of Tibet. He was given the Congressional Gold Medal by President Bush in 2007. The Dalai Lama has declared that Tibet wants autonomy, not independence. However, the Chinese distrust him, believing that he has not really given up the quest for Tibetan independence. Talks between representatives of the Dalai Lama and the Chinese government began in May, 2008 brought little result. China under Xi Jinping has consolidated its military hold on Tibet. He is supposed to be planning to obliterate the Tibetan people and culture in the same way as he is dealing with the Uighurs of Xinjiang. The world and the Indian Government look on and make sympathetic noises.

Summary

Tibet was an independent nation till it was conquered by the Mongols in 1244. There after it became a colony of the Chinese Yuan Dynasty and the Qing Dynasty. Tibet under the Dalai Lamas were allowed autonomy in religious and local affair. This ended in 1571 when the Qing Dynasty appointed a council to rule Tibet. In between, **Tibet enjoyed de facto independence whenever the Chinese Government became weak.** This happened during the power struggle after the fall of the Yuan and the Qing Dynasties.

The boundaries between Ladakh and Tibet were first laid down in the treaty of Treaty of Tingmosang, 1684. The same were accepted after the Sino-Sikh war of 1842.

The boundary between Tibet and India in the east, McMohan Line, was laid down at the Shimla Convention of 1912-13. It was recognized by Tibet but not by China.

Today, the nation of Tibet does not exist. **Not one foreign government officially recognizes the Tibetan government in exile.** Even India recognizes that Tibet is an integral part of China. But China is suspicious of Indian and western designs.

Geopolitical situations keep changing. **China apprehends that India and the west may support a struggle for independence in Tibet.** In 2006, the Dalai Lama has declared that "Tibet wants autonomy, not independence." However, the Chinese distrust him, believing that he has not really given up the quest for Tibetan independence. **Projects such as the Qinghai – Tibet Railway have roused fears of facilitating military mobilization and Han migration.** Both have since become a reality.

China is paranoid about the Dalai Lama and his hold on the Tibetan people. The Chinese fear that the Tibetan exiles in India may one day restart an armed freedom struggle in Tibet with Indian and Western assistance. **Dalai Lama and the Tibetan people in India remains a major and difficult issue in Sino Indian relations.**

Analysis

Tibet was an independent country till 1244. There after it became a Chinese colony. **Does a colonial power have the right to claim perpetual right to colonize? Europe was once a colony of Rome. Does that give the right to Italy to perpetually colonise Europe? India was once a British Colony. Did it not fight the colonial power and gain independence. Every colony has the right to independence. It is the duty of the UN and the free** world to enforce this right.

CHAPTER TWO

India's Relations with China

Relations Before 1950

Both India and China are large, ancient nations whose history dates back almost 5000 years. There is a long history of trade and cultural exchanges between the two countries. **But there was hardly any military conflict between the two. This was perhaps due to the fact that Tibet was an independent country till 1244. Thereafter, the formidable Karakorum and Himalayan ranges which made large scale military expeditions unsustainable.** Relations between India and China were indirect till 1244. Since Tibet was colonized by China in 1244, direct relations between India and China started. However, prior to 1950, relations mainly pertain to India's relations with an autonomous Tibet.

1950 - 1984

The "People's Republic of China (PRC)" was established in 1950. India was the 16th state to establish diplomatic relations with it. Mao Zedong, the Chairman of the Communist Party of China viewed Tibet as an integral part of the Chinese State. **Mao was determined to bring Tibet under direct administrative and military control of PRC.** It considered Indian concern over human rights violations in Tibet as an interference by the Indian Government in the internal affairs of the PRC. The PRC took control over Tibet and ended Dalai Lama's domination by force of arms in 1950. **To avoid antagonizing China, Nehru informed Chinese leaders that India did not have any political or territorial ambitions in Tibet.** With Indian support, Tibetan delegates signed an agreement in May 1951 recognizing PRC sovereignty but guaranteeing that the existing political and social system of Tibet would continue.

Nehru had dreamt of Sino-Indian friendship. He spelt out the "five principles of peaceful co-existence" between the two countries in the "Panchasheel Treaty" of 1954. The catch phrase of India's diplomacy with

China in the 1950s was *"Hindi-Chini bhai-bhai"*, which means that Indians and Chinese are brothers. In 1954, India published new maps that included the Aksai Chin region within the boundaries of India. Then an Indian reconnaissance party of Indian border police discovered a completed Chinese road running through the Aksai Chin region. Border clashes and Indian protests became more frequent and serious. **In January 1959, PRC premier Zhou Enlai wrote to Nehru, rejecting Nehru's contention that the border was based on any existing treaty and custom and pointed out that no government in China had ever accepted the McMohan Line, which defined the eastern section of the border between India and Tibet as legal. China claimed 104,000 square km of territory over which India's maps showed clear sovereignty and demanded "rectification" of the entire border.** Zhou Enlai proposed that China would relinquish its claim to most of India's north-east in exchange for India's abandonment of its claim to Aksai Chin. The Indian government, constrained by domestic public opinion, rejected the idea of a settlement based on uncompensated loss of territory as being humiliating and unequal.

Relations between the two countries further soured in 1959 when Tibetan spiritual leader Dalai Lama fled communist persecution and was given asylum in India with 15,000 of his followers. Soon after, the border dispute worsened between the two countries. China claimed Aksai Chin in the western sector and India claimed territories south of the McMahon line in the eastern sector. **Some retired government servants have suggested that India failed to avail of a great opportunity of settling the border question at the time of Chinese Premier Zhou Enlai's visit to New Delhi in April 1960 when the Chinese were also keen to close the issue. They do not dwell on the fact that this could only have been achieved if India had ceded all the territories which China had quietly annexed in Ladakh between 1950 and 1960 and also Tawang. Sections of the Congress party along with Opposition MPs like Atal Bihari Vajpayee opposed the move.**

Border disputes resulted in a short border war between the People's Republic of China and India. The war started on 20th October 1962. Within a few weeks, the Chinese Army pushed the ill prepared and inadequately led Indian forces to within forty-eight kms of the Assam plains. They consolidated their hold on Aksai Chin and occupied strategic points in Ladakh. China declared a unilateral cease fire on 21 November 1962 and withdrew twenty kms behind the actual line of control. Indians believe that India was attacked by China in 1962. However, Neville Maxwell in his books

"India's China War" held India primarily responsible for the border war. Indian authorities have never accepted this in public, although privately his views have considerable support amongst Indian scholars and experts.

Relations between the PRC and India deteriorated during the rest of the 1960s and the early 1970s. China diplomatically backed Pakistan in its 1965 war with India. Between 1967 and 1971, an all-weather road was built in Pakistan Occupied Kashmir (POK) linking China's Xinjiang Province with Pakistan. India could do no more than protest. **China supplied ideological, financial and other assistance to dissident groups, especially to Naga insurgents in north eastern India.** China also accused India of assisting the Khampa rebels in Tibet. Diplomatic contact between the two governments was minimal although not formally severed. Border clashes continued to occur. **In late 1967, there were two skirmishes between Indian and Chinese forces in Sikkim. The first one was dubbed the "Nathu La incident", and the other the "Chola incident".**

China did not attack Sikkim in 1962. One reason could be that the logistics required to fight a war was not in place. It is also possible that it did not have resources to attack on so many fronts. **In late 1967, there were two skirmishes between Indian and Chinese forces in Sikkim.** On 11th September 1967, troops of the Indian Army's 18th Rajput Regiment were protecting an Engineering Company that was fencing the border at Nathu La when Chinese troops opened fire on them. This incident escalated over the next five days to an exchange of heavy artillery and mortar fire between the Indians and the Chinese. **62 Indian soldiers, from the 18th Rajput, the 2nd Grenadiers and the Artillery regiments were killed. Major Harbhajan Singh of the Rajput Regiment was awarded a Mahavir Chakra (posthumous) and Naib Subedar Pandey a Vir Chakra (posthumous) for their gallant actions. The extent of Chinese casualties in this incident is not known but high enough for them to back off.**

On 1 October 1967, a group of Indian soldiers noticed Chinese troops surrounding a forward post at the Cho La outpost on Sikkim Tibet border. After a heated argument over the control of the area, a Chinese soldier bayoneted a Gurkha rifleman, triggering the start of a close quarters knife and fire fight, which then escalated to a mortar and heavy machine gun duel. The Chinese troops signaled a ceasefire after three hours of fighting but later scaled Point 15450 to establish them there. The Gurkhas outflanked them the next day to regain Point 15450 and the Chinese retreated across the Line of Actual Control (LAC). **21 Indian soldiers were killed in this** action. The Indian government awarded Vir Chakras to Rifleman Limbu (posthumous) and battalion commander Major K.B. Joshi for their gallant actions. The extent of Chinese casualties in this skirmish were enough for them to pull back.

India and China made efforts to improve relations after 1979. China remained silent on India's annexation of Sikkim and its special relationship with Bhutan. The Chinese leaders agreed to discuss the boundary issue. Mount Kailash and Mansarovar Lake in Tibet were opened to annual pilgrimages from India. In 1980, Indian Prime Minister Indira Gandhi approved a plan to upgrade the deployment of forces around the Line of Actual Control to avoid unilateral redefinitions of the line. India also increased funds for infrastructure development in these areas.

1984 - 2003

In 1984, squads of Indian soldiers began actively patrolling the Sumdorong Chu Valley in Arunachal Pradesh. They area was claimed by both sides. The Indian team had left the area before the winter. **In the winter of 1986, the Chinese deployed their troops to the Sumdorong Chu before the Indian team could arrive in the summer and built a helipad at Wandung. Surprised by the Chinese occupation, Indian Army airlifted a brigade to the region.** Chinese troops could not move any further into the valley and were forced to move sideways along the Thag La ridge, away from the valley. India granted of statehood to Arunachal Pradesh in February 1987. This angered China. Both sides deployed new troops to the area, raising tensions and fears of a new border war. China sent out warnings that it would "teach India a lesson" if it did not cease "nibbling" at Chinese territory. Both sides had backed away from conflict by the summer of 1987and denied that military clashes had taken place. Indian foreign minister and Prime Minister traveled to Beijing in 1988 and negotiated a mutual de-escalation. Relations remained cordial.

India and China held eight rounds of border negotiations between December 1981 and November 1987. These talks initially raised hopes that progress could be made on the border issue. However, in 1985 the Chinese stiffened their position on the border and wanted concessions without defining the exact terms of its "package proposal" or where the actual line of control (LAC) lay. India granted of statehood to Arunachal Pradesh in February 1987. This caused both sides to deploy new troops to the area, raising tensions and fears of a new border war. The PRC relayed warnings that it would "teach India a lesson" if it did not cease "nibbling" at Chinese territory. By the summer of 1987, however, both sides had backed away from conflict and denied that military clashes had taken place.

Improvement in relations between the two countries was facilitated by Rajeev Gandhi's visit to China in December 1988. It was the first visit by an Indian prime minister to China since Nehru's 1954 visit. The two sides issued a joint communique that stressed the need to restore friendly relations on the basis of the principles of "Panch Sheel". India and the People's Republic of China agreed to broaden bilateral ties in various areas and work to achieve a "fair and reasonable settlement while seeking a mutually acceptable solution" to the border dispute. **The communique also expressed China's concern about agitation by Tibetan separatists in India and reiterated China's position that Tibet was an integral part of China.** Rajeev Gandhi signed bilateral agreements on cooperation in science and technology, on civil aviation to establish direct air links and on cultural exchanges. The two sides also agreed to hold annual diplomatic consultations between foreign ministers and to set up a joint ministerial committee on economic and scientific cooperation and a joint working group on the boundary issue. The latter group was to be led by the Indian foreign secretary and the Chinese vice minister of foreign affairs.

The mid-1990s showed a slow but steady improvement in relations with China. Top level dialog continued with the December 1991 visit of Chinese premier Li Peng to India and the May 1992 visit to China of Indian President R Venkataraman. Progress was also made in reducing tensions on the border via confidence-building measures, including mutual troop reductions, regular meetings of local military commanders and advance notification of military exercises. **Border trade resumed in July 1992 after a gap of more than thirty years. Consulates reopened in Mumbai and Shanghai in 1992. The two sides agreed to open an additional border trading post in 1993.**

Prime Minister Narsimha Rao and Premier Li Peng signed the border agreement and three other agreements on cross-border trade, on increased cooperation on environment and in radio and television broadcasting during the formers visit to Beijing in September 1993. A senior level Chinese military delegation made a six-day goodwill visit to India in December 1993. India ignored reports that China was exporting greater amounts of military material to Burma's army, navy and air force and sending an increasing number of technicians to Burma. **Indian authorities also played down the presence of Chinese radar technicians in Burma's**

Coco Islands, which border the Andaman and Nicobar Islands. The 1993 Chinese military delegation's visit to India was reciprocated by Indian army chief of staff in 1994. The border issue was raised in September 1994 when Chinese defence minister visited New Delhi for extensive talks with high-level Indian trade and defence officials. Further talks were held in New Delhi in March 1995 by the India-China Expert Group. The two sides were reported to be "seriously engaged" in defining the McMahon Line and the LAC. In January 1994 Beijing announced that it not only favoured a negotiated solution on the Kashmir Issue but also opposed any form of independence for the region. Mr. George Fernandes, then defence minister visited China in 1996. Zhang Zemin, the chairman of the Central Military Commission in 1996, greeted Mr. Fernandes in an unprecedented gesture. In December 1996, President Jiang Zemin most unexpectedly told his Pakistani hosts that India and Pakistan must set aside their differences and foster an economic relationship. During the Kargil war, the Chinese stance was a tacit acceptance of the LOC in Jammu and Kashmir as the international border.

India China relations nosedived again in May 1998 after India conducted nuclear tests. Some believe that Mr. Vajpayee as Prime Minister wrote to President Bill Clinton pointing to China as the reason for India going nuclear. Mr. George Fernandes was widely quoted as having said that China is India's enemy number one. But he consistently denied ever having made such a statement. India also accused China of supporting Pakistan's nuclear and missile programs. Relations between India and China stayed strained until the end of the decade.

Indian President K R Narayana visited China in 2000. This marked a gradual diplomatic re-engagement of India and China. In a major embarrassment for China, the 17th Karamapa, Urggyen Trinley Dorje, who was proclaimed by China, made a dramatic escape from Tibet to the Rumtak Monastery in Sikkim. Chinese officials were in a quandary on this issue as any protest to India on the issue would mean an explicit endorsement on India's governance of Sikkim, which the Chinese still hadn't recognized. **In 2002, Chinese Premier Zhu Rongji reciprocated the President's visit by visiting India with a focus on economic issues. 2003 ushered in a marked improvement in Sino-Indian relations following Indian Prime Minister Atal Bihari Vajpayee's visit to China in June 2003. China officially recognized Indian sovereignty over Sikkim as the two nations moved toward resolving their border disputes.**

2004 - 2014

2004 also witnessed a gradual improvement in relations. The Nathu La and Jelep La passes in Sikkim were opened for border trade. 2004 was a milestone in Sino-Indian bilateral trade which surpassed the $10 billion mark for the first time. **In April 2005, Chinese Premier Wen Jiabao visited Bangalore to push for increased Sino-Indian cooperation in high-tech industries.** The high-level visit produced several agreements to deepen political, cultural and economic ties between the two nations. But China has not supported India on the issue of India gaining a permanent seat on the UN Security Council. China was granted an observer status in the SAARC Summit of 2005. While other countries in the region are ready to consider China for permanent membership in the SAARC, India is reluctant.

In November 2006, China and India had a verbal spat over claim of the north eastern Indian state of Arunachal Pradesh. India claimed that China was occupying 38,000 sq km of its territory in Kashmir, while China claimed the whole of Arunachal Pradesh as its own. In May 2007, China denied the application for visa from an IAS officer from Arunachal Pradesh. According to China, since Arunachal Pradesh is a territory of China, he did not need a visa to visit his own country. Later in December 2007, China appeared to have reversed its policy by granting the visa. to Marpe Sora, an Arunachal born professor in computer science. In January 2008, Prime Minister Manmohan Singh visited China and met with President Hu Jintao and Premier Wen Jibao and had bilateral discussions related to trade, commerce, defence, military and various other issues.

On Jan. 14, 2008, during his first official visit to Beijing, India Prime Minister Manmohan Singh sat down with Chinese Premier Wen Jiabao in the Great Hall of the People to emphasize what the two Asian giants have in common. The leaders signed a seven-page document that covers issues such as their fast-growing economic ties, defence cooperation, anti-terrorism efforts, climate change and energy policies. Noting that India and China "are the two largest developing nations on earth representing more than one-third of humanity," the document goes on to note that the countries with a history of mutual suspicion are now "convinced that it is time to look to the future in building a relationship," and that "China India friendship and common development will have a positive influence on the future of the world."

2014 to Date

BJP came to power in 2014 and Mr. Narendra Modi became Prime Minister. **Mr. Modi tried to improve relations with China. He invited the Chinese President Xi Jinping to his home state, Gujarat. The Chinese President reciprocated the gesture by inviting Mr. Modi. However, the bonhomie remained visual.China has stubbornly refused to allow India entry into the Nuclear Suppliers Group.** It has vetoed UN proposal to declare Mumbai terror attack mastermind Hafeez Saeed a global terrorist. Under Xi, China has displayed strong expansionist tendencies in South China Sea and against India. It has given Tibetan names to six towns in Arunachal Pradesh in its maps. **The standoff between the two armies at Doka La pass and Dokalam Plateau in Chumbi Valley of Tibet show no sign of ending.** Dokalam plateau is recognized by India as belonging to Bhutan. Since India is treaty bound to protect Bhutan, it has troops deployed at Doka La and Dokalam. China claims that Dokalam belongs to it and not to Bhutan. As per China's new assertive and aggressive policy it started building a road in the region and destroyed two India bunkers at Doka La. Indian troops have physically pushed the Chinese back.

Beginning on 5 May 2020, Chinese and Indian troops were engaged in a face-off at locations along LAC in Ladakh. In late May, Chinese forces objected to Indian road construction in the Galwan River valley. Chinese and Indian troops clashed on 15/16 June 2020. **The incident resulted in the deaths of 20 Indian soldiers. Casualties on the Chinese side was not declared. On 7 September, shots were fired along the LAC for the first time in 45 years.** Both sides blamed each other for the incident. Partial disengagement from Galwan, Hot Springs, and Gogra occurred in June–July 2020. Complete disengagement from Pangong Lake north and south bank took place in February 2021. **It has changed the status quo on the North Bank of Pangong Tso.** It tried to capture heights on the south bank of Pangong Tso and were thwarted by timely occupation of the features like Gurung Hill and Rezangla. It has been building new military infrastructures like airfields, radar installations, missile bases, ammunition and logistic depots and accommodation for troops all along the LAC from Ladakh to Arunachal. It is now building a bridge across Pangong Tso in disputed territory since the 1962 War. It has launched many propaganda videos displaying the fire power of its weapon systems in a bid to cow down Indians. **Fourteen rounds of talks between military commanders and leaders have not resultant in de-escalation and disengagement of the armies of the two sides. Chinese media is threatening war. Chinese**

ambassador is talking tough. Indian Army Chief says that his defence forces are ready to meet any Chinese aggression. It seems India has decided to play the waiting game. In the mean time we continue to trade with China. Our trade deficit continues to fund China's growing defence budget.

The Border Dispute

First let us see the **problems on the Western Borders** which extend from Daulat Beg Oldie in Western Ladakh to the Spiti in Uttarakhand. As explained in Chapter 1, the Chinese and the Sikhs signed a treaty in September 1842, which laid down the boundary between Ladakh and Tibet. The sovereignty of Ladakh was transferred to the British when they defeated the Sikhs in 1846. The border was defined by natural features and never demarcated. The points at the two extremities of the disputed boundary in Ladakh, Demchok and Karakorum Pass, were well defined, but **the Aksai Chin area which lay in between these two features lay undefined.** W. H. Johnson, an officer with the Survey of India, proposed the "Johnson Line" as border between Ladakh and Tibet in 1865. This line puts Aksai Chin in Kashmir. This line was never presented to the Chinese for ratification. **Johnson presented this line to the Maharaja of Kashmir, who then claimed the 38,000 sq km territory.By 1892, China had erected border trading posts at Karakorum Pass and Khunjareb Pass.** At this time, Britain and China were allies and Britain was principally concerned that Aksai Chin does not fall into Russian hands. **When China showed an interest in Aksai Chin, Britain proposed a revised boundary, called the McCartney-Macdonald Line, which puts most of Aksai Chin in Chinese territory. This line ran along the Karakorum Mountains.** The Karakorum Mountains formed a natural boundary up to the Indus River watershed. It left the Tarim River basin in Chinese control. **In 1899, the British presented this line to the Chinese, who raised no objection to it. This line is approximately the same as the current Line of Actual Control.** Both lines were used on British maps of India. Central power in China collapsed in 1911 with the collapse of the Manchu Qing Dynasty and Tibet declared independence. **At the end of World War I, the British officially used the Johnson Line in their maps.** But they took no steps to establish outposts or assert actual control on the ground. **In 1927, the border was adjusted again as the British Government in India abandoned the Johnson line in favour of the McCartney-Macdonald Line along the Karakorum range further south. However, the maps were not updated and still showed the Johnson Line.** The boundary remained un-demarcated at India's independence.

After independence in 1947, the Indian government used the Johnson Line as the basis for its official boundary in the west. Thus, the Aksai Chin area became a part of India on its maps. In July 1954, Prime Minister Nehru directed that the maps of India be revised to show definite boundaries on all frontiers. Up to this point, the boundary in the Aksai Chin sector, based on the Johnson Line, had been described as "un-demarcated.". During the 1950s, China built a 1,200 km road connecting Xinjiang Province and western Tibet. Of this 179 km ran south of the Johnson Line through the Aksai Chin region claimed by India. Aksai Chin was easily accessible to the Chinese, but was more difficult for the Indians on the other side of the Karakorum to reach. The Indians did not learn of the existence of the road until 1957. The road was confirmed when it was shown in Chinese maps published in 1958. In October 13, 1962, China and Pakistan began negotiations over the boundary west of the Karakorum Pass and in 1963, the two countries settled their boundaries largely on the basis of the McCartney-Macdonald Line.

The Indian position, as stated by prime minister Jawaharlal Nehru was that the Aksai Chin was "part of the Ladakh region of India for centuries" and that this northern border was a "firm and definite one which was not open to discussion with anybody". The Chinese prime minister, Zhou Enlai argued that the western border had never been demarcated, that the McCartney-Macdonald Line, which left the Aksai Chin within Chinese borders was the only line ever proposed to a Chinese government and that the Aksai Chin was already under Chinese jurisdiction and that negotiations should take into account the status quo.

There is some dispute in the areas of upper Kinnaur in Himachal Pradesh and Spiti in Uttarakhand. These areas had been parts of the Tibetan Kingdom of Guge Puran. They were captured by the British and hence considered India territory.

India considers the McMohan Line as its boundary with China in the east. The British annexed Assam and the north eastern states by the Treaty of Yandaboo at the conclusion of the First Anglo Burmese War in 1826. This resulted in India and China having a common border other than India's border with Tibet. In 1913-14, representatives of Britain, China, and Tibet attended a conference in Shimla, India and drew up an agreement concerning Tibet's status and borders. The McMahon Line, a proposed boundary between Tibet, China and India for the eastern sector, was drawn by British negotiator Henry McMahon on a map attached to the agreement. All three representatives initialled the agreement, but Beijing immediately objected to the proposed Sino-Tibet boundary and repudiated the agreement. Some reports suggest that McMahon had been instructed not to sign the treaty bilaterally with Tibetans if China refused, but he did so without the Chinese representative present and then kept the declaration secret. **China claims that by signing the Simla Agreement with Tibet, the British had violated the Anglo-Chinese Convention of 1906, which bound the British government "not to annex Tibetan territory."** Because of doubts concerning the legal status of the accord, the British did not put the McMahon Line on their maps until 1937, nor did they publish the Simla Convention in the treaty record until 1938. Indian government held the view that the Himalayas were the ancient boundaries of the Indian subcontinent and thus should be the boundaries of British India and later independent India.

China argued that the Shimla Convention and McMahon Line were illegal and that Tibet was not an independent country in 1913 and did not have any treaty making powers. Tibetan officials continued to administer Tawang and refused to concede the territory during negotiations in 1938. The situation remained the same till the British annexed Tawang region during World War II. In 1947, Tibet requested that India recognize Tibetan authority over Tawang, south of the McMahon Line. This was rejected.

China's claim on areas south of the McMahon Line, encompassing Arunachal Pradesh, were based on traditional boundaries between India and Tibet. India believes that the boundaries China proposed in Ladakh and Arunachal Pradesh have no written basis and no documentation of acceptance by anyone apart from China. **Indians argue that China claims the territory on the basis that it was under Chinese imperial control in the past, while Chinese argue that India claims the territory on the basis that it was under British imperial control in the past.** India claims that the intent of the treaty of 1913 was to follow the highest ridges of the Himalayas while demarcating the border. They claimed that South of the highest ridges should be Indian territory and North of the highest ridges should be Chinese territory. In the Indian claim, the two armies would be separated from each other by the highest mountains in the world. Parts of India's claim line in the eastern sector follow a modified version of the McMahon Line. The original line drawn up by Henry McMahon on the Shimla Treaty map starts at 27°44'30"N, starting a tri-junction between

Bhutan, China and India and from there, extends eastwards. Starting from the 1950s, when India began patrolling this area, they found that they at multiple locations, the highest ridges fell north of the McMahon Line as shown in the treaty map and their own maps and they modified their maps to extend the boundary northwards to include features such as Thag La, Longju, and Khinzemane as Indian territories. Thus, the Indian version of the McMahon Line moves the Bhutan-China-India tri junction north to 27°48'N. India claims that the treaty map ran along features such as Thag La, though the actual treaty map itself is topographically vague (as the treaty was not accompanied with demarcation). The treaty includes no verbal description of geographic features nor description of the highest ridges.

China's Counter India Strategy

Beijing's "counter-India" strategy was drawn up in the 1950s. India was identified as an eventual competitor for being the pre-eminent power in Asia. The strategy is to encircle India by a ring of countries friendly to China and inject in them fears of the Indian threat. That is why China embarked on a long-term propaganda or psychological warfare employing its official media, military strategic experts and political scientists to project the "India Threat" theory among India's neighbours. **China aligned with Pakistan as early as 1963** and has been a major supplier of military equipment, technology and economic aid since then. It next **aligned with Bangladesh in 1976** and was during the BNP Regime the primary supplier of military equipment and aid to Bangladesh. However, with change in political power in Bangladesh, Chinese influence in Bangladesh has waned. It next **aligned with the Military Junta ruling Myanmar in 1988.** Chinese military and economic aid have enabled the Military Junta in Myanmar to defy the US and the West and continue with its autocratic regime. **China aligned with Sri Lanka in its battle with the LTTE in 2004.** It has supplied military equipment and aid to Sri Lanka and encouraged Pakistan to do the same. It is providing economic aid and assisting Sri Lanka in developing its infrastructure and oil and gas resources. **It has increased its influence in Nepal with the Communists coming to power.** Bhutan is the only SAARC nation other than India which will not be in the Chinese camp. China is known to have denied India membership of the APEC. It also tried to keep India outside the ASEAN and the ASEAN Regional Forum (ARF). It opposes India getting a seat in the UN Security Council.

Indo – US Defence Cooperation

Beijing makes no secret of its perception that it considers India to be a part of US plans to encircle China. China believes that the Indo-US defence cooperation was to counter China's regional aspirations and the US intended to form a strategic partnership with India to increase its influence in South Asia to counter China. It also considers that the US-India nuclear co-operation was part of India's ambition to become a super power and its conventional defence build-up was aimed to dominate South Asia. India's membership of QUAD and military and economic relations with Vietnam, Taiwan and Philippines has made China more hostile.

Summary

Historical relations between India and China have been largely restricted to trade and cultural exchanges. But **post 1950, their relations have been plagued by border disputes, Tibet and regional rivalry.** There are some issues between the two countries which are difficult to resolve.

The first and most pressing problem is the territorial dispute. Both neighbours claim that the other occupies territory that is rightfully theirs.

The second insolvable problem is the presence of Dalai Lama and Tibetan refugees in India. China sees these people as a potential threat to its hold over Tibet. It is impossible for India to deport Dalai Lama and the Tibetan refugees to Tibet.

There are other problems too. **India cannot ignore of China's military alliances with Pakistan, Bangladesh, Sri Lanka, Myanmar and Nepal.**

China has its own worries. It was none too pleased with the QUAD, an alliance of USA, Japan, Australia and India created by President Donald Trump to preserve South China Sea as international waters. Beijing believes the close co-operation between these four countries was directed against China. India's growing closeness to the U.S., including the India-U.S. nuclear cooperation, has made China nervous.

Relations between China and India are at its worst in recent years. The bonhomie between Mr. Modi and Mr. Xi Jinping of 2014 has not endured. The armies of the two countries are in eyeball-to-eyeball contact in Ladakh and in high state of alert in other areas. War can break out at any moment.

China under Xi Jinping has passed a new law making it territorial claims non-negotiable. There is no possibility of resolving the boundary issue unless both countries are ready to accept the LAC as the international border. As of today, this is highly unlikely. In fact, the indications are quite to the contrary.

Analysis

India cannot prevent China from being friendly with its neighbours and providing them with military equipment, military and economic aid. No amount of sugar coating or rhetoric can hide the insurmountable nature of the problems to friendly relations between the two countries. **One option before India is to make itself militarily and economically strong enough to make China averse to a military adventure against it.**

The second is to liberate Tibet, not by a military offensive; but by providing military and economic aid to Tibetans, within and outside Tibet, who are ready to fight and liberate Tibet. Thiswouldbe a fitting reply to China which has been providing military and economic aid to Naga, Mizo, ULFA andother insurgent groups of the North East since 1950 and its support to Pakistan based terrorist operating in J&K at the UN.

CHAPTER THREE

China's Intentions and Capabilities

Chinese Intentions

All ambiguity about Chinese intentions of solving its border disputes with its neighbours is over. President Xi Jinping has passed a new border law that lays down how China is going to secure its borders. The new law has been in effect since January 1, 2022.

The Standing Committee of the National People's Congress, China's top legislative body, passed a new law on October 23, 2021laying down the law for "protection and exploitation of the country's land border areas". The law is not meant specifically for the border with India. China has about 22,500 km land boundary with 14 countries including India. The new Law has 62 articles and seven chapters. Some salient features are given in the succeeding paragraphs.

As per the law, the People's Republic of China shall set up boundary markers on all its land borders to clearly mark the border. The type of marker is to be decided in agreement with the neighbouring country in question. It will be clear that China is likely to dig in its heels at the current disputed positions at the LAC and will construct more dual-purpose model border villages which can be used both for military and civilian purposes.

The law further stated that People's Liberation Army (PLA) and Chinese People's Armed Police Force will maintain security along the border. This responsibility includes cooperating with local authorities in combating illegal border crossings.

The law prohibits any party from indulging in any activity in the border area which would "endanger national security or affect China's friendly relations with neighbouring countries". It includes construction of any permanent buildings by any person without authorisation from the concerned authority.

The Law further it states that citizens and local organisations are mandated to protect and defend the border infrastructure, maintain security and stability of borders and co-operate with government agencies in maintaining border security. The law lays down the path for the development of the border region. It states that People's Republic of China will take up education and propaganda to "solidify the sense of community of China, to promote the spirit of China, to defend the unity and territorial integrity of the country, strengthen citizens' sense of the country and homeland security, and build a common spiritual home for the Chinese nation" amongst citizens in the border region.

The Law permits the Chinese State to take measures "to strengthen border defence, support economic and social development as well as opening-up in border areas, improve public services and infrastructure in such areas, encourage and support people's life and work there, and promote coordination between border defence and social, economic development in border areas". In other words, the encourages the Chinese Government to settle civilians in the border areas and thereby consolidate territorial claims.

The new land border law is a clear attempt by China to unilaterally delineate and demarcate territorial boundaries with India and Bhutan. The territorial disputes are now non-negotiable. India, Nepal, Bhutan and other countries will have to accept Chinese claims or be ready to fight. As a follow up of the law, China renamed 15 places of Arunachal Pradesh in their map on December 30, 2021. The Law paves the way for enabling China to take over illegal control of sovereign territories of other countries.

The Indian people and the Indian Government need to understand and accept that all military and diplomatic discussions with the Chinese about territorial disputes with China are useless.It is Chinese solution or no solution. India must either give in to Chinese demands or get ready to fight. It will be naïve to think that China will immediately launch attacks to take territories they claim. They will use threats and propaganda to encourage its enemies to give up without a fight. **Grandpa hopes that Indian Government will not surrender without a fight.**

Chinese Armed Forces

China's armed forces are ranked the largest in the world with a combined strength of about 2.2 million men at arms and about one million reserves. It had a **military budget of US $209 in 2020, which is second only**

to the US. India in comparison had a budget of only about US $ 54 billion 2021-22.

In the last twenty years it has gone all out to modernize its forces. **The regular army has been reduced by about 500,000 men over the past few years with the 500,000** being transferred to Armed Police Divisions which have been deployed on its borders. Combat effectiveness is sought to be increased by technology-intensive elements such as special forces, army aviation (transport aircraft and helicopters), surface to air missiles (SAM) and electronic warfare units. **The latest operational doctrine of the PLA ground forces highlights the importance of information technology, electronic and cyber warfare and long-range precision missile strikes in future wars. The older generation command, control, and communications (C3) systems are being replaced by an integrated battlefield information networks featuring local/wide-area networks (LAN/WAN), satellite communications, unmanned aerial vehicle (drone) based surveillance and reconnaissance systems and mobile command and control centres.** Russian exports latest technology and weapons systems to China. However, modernization of a large force as that of China requires time and money. So, the Chinese formations are classified as Category A or Category B. Category A formations have priority for modernization.

Chinese Regular Army

China has the world's largest ground forces, currently totalling some 1.6 million personnel. The Chinese regular army consists of 18 Group Armies, which are comparable to Indian "corps" size combined arms formations. According to the International Institute of Strategic Studies' 2006 Military Balance Report, China has nine armoured divisions, three mechanized infantry divisions, twenty four motorized infantry divisions, fifteen infantry divisions, two amphibious assault divisions, one mechanized infantry brigade, twenty two motorized infantry brigades, twelve armoured brigades, seven artillery divisions, fourteen artillery brigades, nineteen anti-aircraft artillery (AAA) missile brigades, and ten army aviation (helicopter) regiments. The ground forces are divided among the seven military regions. The allotment of troops to the military regions keeps changing depending on operational requirements.

Shenyang Military Region is located at the North East corner of China and is responsible for defending its borders with Russian Federation and North Korea. This region has only one group army, the 16th Army Group and three military districts.

Beijing Military Region is responsible for the borders with Mongolia and Russia. It could be holding some of the Chinese strategic reserves. It has four Army groups armies, three military districts and two garrisons one of which is located in Beijing. It could be having some independent divisions.

Jinan Military Region lies on China's east coast between the Beijing Military Region and the Nanjing Military Region. It is not located on any international border and could be holding Chinese strategic reserves. This region has two army groups and two military districts.

Nanjing Military Region lies on the east coast of China and is responsible for operations against Taiwan. It has four group armies and a concentration of offensive formations and amphibious capabilities. This region has four Group Armies, five military districts and the Shanghai garrison.

Guangzhou Military Region is one of the smallest military regions in terms of area. It is responsible for operations in Hong Kong, Macao and a part of China's border with Vietnam. It is also closest to Arunachal after Chengdu Military region and could provide troops for operations against India. It has two group armies, the details of which are given below. It also has four military districts and the Hong Kong and Macau garrisons.

Chengdu Military Region is responsible for China's borders with India, Nepal, Bhutan, Burma and a part of Vietnam and internal security of Tibetan Autonomous Region. As such this military region is of most interest to India. This Military operation is responsible for operation against India. The region has three group armies and a number of independent holding units and armed police units permanently deployed in Tibet. The details of Chinese troops deployed in Tibet is discussed in Chapter 9. The details of troops in Chengdu military region are given below. The region also has four military districts and the Chongqing garrison.

Lanzhou Military Region is located in the north west areas of China. It is responsible for defence of international borders with India (North Kashmir), Pakistan (POK), Afghanistan, Kyrgyzstan, Kazakhstan and Mongolia. **It is also responsible for internal security of Xinjiang Province including Aksai Chin andhandling the standoff in Ladakh**

Qinghai Provinces. This military region has two Group Armies and five Military districts.

The regular army units are sometimes used for internal security duties like quelling the student demonstrations at the Tianaman Square and

Tibetan protests in Tibet and Xinjiang Provinces. They are also used in aid to civil authorities at times of natural disasters like earthquakes or floods.

Reserves

In times of crisis, the Chinese Army will be reinforced by activating numerous reserve units and paramilitary units. The PLA reserve component has about 1.2 to1.5 million personnel.

Equipment

The Chinese produced Type 59 and Type 69 tanks (equivalent to Soviet T54 and T55) account for over two-thirds of the total PLA tank inventory. Second generation tanks such as the Type 88 and Type 96 have also been introduced. The latest tank is the Type 99 which entered PLA service in 2001. The PLA also operates about 2,000 light tanks including the Type 62 light tank and the Type 63 amphibious tank. The Type 63 has now been upgraded. The total tank strength is estimated to be about 7500. China also has a large number of wheeled and tracked armoured personnel carriers (APCs) of both indigenous and Soviet manufacture. The fleet includes BMP1, BMP2, BMP3, Nornico Type 89, Type 93, BTR 80 and BTR 152 armoured personnel carriers.

The artillery includes indigenously produced 105mm and 122mm howitzers, multi barrel rocket launchers, HN5A surface to air missiles. Infantry units are equipped with indigenously produced 60mm and 120mm mortars, and 57mm, 76mm, 106mm antitank weapons and the Red Arrow anti tank missiles.

PLA's Fighting Prowess

The Korean War was the first war fought by China after independence. In 1950, the PLA attacked the US forces in the Korean Peninsula in support of North Korea. At this stage, the PLA was battle hardened due to China's long conflict with Japanese occupation, World War II and civil war with Nationalists. **The PLA suffered heavy casualties but fought the technologically superior US armed forces, who had total air superiority, with skill and determination and brought them to a standstill.**

The Sino Indian conflict of 1962 was the next war PLA fought. In October 1962, the PLA routed the Indian Army in Ladakh and Arunachal and declared unilateral ceasefire after taking possession of over 30,000 sq. km of Indian territory in about a month of fighting. **The Chinese success was largely due to the total unpreparedness of the Indian Army and exceptionally poor Indian military leadership. It was also due to a total failure of the political leadership of India and government of India to** assess correctly the PLA's capabilities and intentions and to build a professional well equipped armed forces that could defend its borders.

The next Chinese military adventure was against India on the Sikkim Tibet border during1965-67. During the period from September to December 1965. The PLA sent a number of probing missions on the entire Sikkim-Tibet border. The Indian Army responded firmly at local levels. Though details of Chinese casualties from these border clashes have not been made public, there were reports indicating that the PLA suffered "heavy" casualties against "moderate" losses by India. Two years later, **in September 1967, the PLA launched a direct attack on the Indian Army units at Nathu La, on the Sikkim-Tibet border. The six-adventure day border skirmish from September 6 to 13, 1967 included exchange of heavy artillery fire.** The PLA soldiers tried to cross the border in large numbers. The attack was repulsed at all points. The Chinese received a severe mauling in the artillery duels. Indian gunners scored several direct hits on Chinese bunkers, including a command post from where the Chinese operations were being directed. The Chinese were reported to have suffered at least twice as many casualties as the Indians in this encounter. The Nathu La episode demonstrated beyond doubt that the PLA was not invincible.

The Sino-Vietnam War of 1979 was the last major Military adventure of the PLA. China wanted "to teach a lesson" to the Vietnamese for their attack on Khmer Rouge in Cambodia in 1978. On 17 February 1979, a PLA force of about 200,000 troops supported by 200 tanks entered northern Vietnam. The PLA invasion was conducted on two fronts. Western front attacked Cao Bang, Lang Son and Quang Ninh Provinces. The Eastern front attacked Ha Tuyen, Hoang Lien Son and Lai Chau Provinces. The PLA met with initial success. The PLA quickly advanced about 15–20 km into Vietnam. The Vietnamese avoided mobilizing their regular divisions and used guerrilla tactics. The initial PLA attack soon lost its momentum. **A new attack wave was launched in with eight PLA divisions joining the battle and succeeded in capturing the heights around Lang Son.** Lang Son fell on 6 March. The PLA attacked Quảng Ninh Province. But they failed to defeat the Vietnamese in the Battle of Mong Cai and Battle of Cao Ba Lanh. **On 6 March, China declared that their punitive mission had been achieved. The PLA crossed the border back into China on 16 March.** Both sides declared victory. Vietnam had quickly mobilized all available forces including some from Cambodia. But they kept their forces for the defence of Hanoi. They claimed to have repelled the invasion using mostly border militias. **Most Western writers agree that Vietnam outperformed the PLA on the battlefield. The Vietnamese claimed that the PLA had suffered over 44,000 casualties. China as usual gave no figures.** As Vietnamese troops remained in Cambodia until 1989, China was unsuccessful in its goal of dissuading Vietnam from involvement in Cambodia. **The defeat made China realize that there was need to improve the fighting capabilities of the PLA. Consequently, the military modernization was accelerated.**

The next Chinese military adventure was against India and is known as the Sumdorong Chu Valley incident of 1986. In mid1986, it came to the notice of India that the PLA had built a helipad at Wandung in Sumdorong Chu Valley in Arunachal Pradesh. India reacted swiftly and the PLA had an eyeball-to-eyeball confrontation with the India Army in Sumdorong Chu Valley in August 1986. After a week of tense moments both sides mutually agreed to withdraw their forces inside their respective territories and create a no man's land.

The current standoff in Ladakh has been deliberately left out as war has not broken out yet. It will thus be seen that the Chinese soldiers are not supermen. But as they say, during wars, God is usually with the side with more and larger guns.

The Chinese Air Force

The Chinese Air Force has about 250,000 personnel and 2300 fighters and ground attack aircrafts. The air force is organized into seven Military Region Air Forces and has 44 Air Divisions. It is the largest air force in Asia-Pacific region and the third largest in the world after the US and Russian Air Forces. An air division has 2 to 3 aviation regiments, each with 20 to 36 aircraft. There are also three air borne divisions manned by the PLAAF. The Chinese Air Force is also divided into 16 Airborne Corps. Shenyang Military has four fighter divisions, two ground attack divisions and a few independent air force regiments. Beijing Military region has three fighter division and one air transport division. Lanzhou military region has two fighter divisions and one bomber division. Nanjing military region has three fighter divisions, one ground attack division and one bomber division. Guangzhou military region has five fighter division, one bomber division and one air transport division. The Jinan military region has two fighter divisions and one ground attack division. The Chengdu military region has only two fighter divisions. In case of a war with India, the air force in Chengdu military region will have to be beefed up with additional air divisions from Lanzhou and Guangzhou military regions.

The Air Force possesses squadrons of F6, F9 and Jian 7 (J7) fighter jets and JY 11-3D air surveillance radars. The JF-10 and J-17 (Thunder) aircraft are the state of art fighters produced in China. Apart from the above there have been acquisitions from Russia including SU-27 aircraft along with production agreement. The best combat aircrafts in China's PLAAF are Russian *SU-30 MK* III and indigenously built, 4th generation *JF 10* and J-17 fighters.

Chinese Navy

China marked the 60th anniversary of the founding of its navy with a spectacular parade in the seas off the northern port city of Qingdao in May 2009. The PLA Navy has about 290,000 personnel. It has a fleet of about 72 combat ships including 26 destroyers, 49 frigates, 14 corvettes, 60 submarines and a large number of fast patrol boats. The government has pushed a vigorous modernization program for the navy. The emphasis is on developing vessels at home or buying them from Russia. It has also built or is planning to build its own submarines, including nuclear-powered ones based on upgraded designs, to replenish its aged fleet. Many of the newer submarines will be based at Hanian, an island province near the recent confrontation between a U.S. navy ship and Chinese warship. (See Map 2). Some of its latest equipment are the Ying Ji missile and C-102 ship-to-ship missiles and the indigenous F 22 P state of art frigate.

Hegemony over South China Sea and conquest of Taiwan remains the focus of Chinese military concerns and its naval strategy. China believes that as its international political and economic stature grows, it must have a navy capable of protecting its expanding global interests. Much of navy's growing budget has gone to building or buying new warships, submarines and other technology required for building a "blue sea navy". Beijing recently demonstrated that ambition by sending warships to help an international effort against pirates menacing commercial ships off the Somali coast. It is seeking to establish its presence in the Indian Ocean by modernizing naval bases at Kyaukpyu, the Coco islands and Sittwe (Akyab) in Myanmar, Chittagong and Kutubdia Island in Bangladesh and Gwadar in Pakistan. It is also improving the Hambantota port in Sri Lanka which could be used as a supply base for the Chinese Navy.

The Chinese Navy is organized into three major fleets, the North Sea Fleet with its headquarters at Qingdao, the East Sea Fleet headquartered at Ningbo, and the South Sea Fleet headquartered in Zhanjiang. The navy includes a Coastal Defence Force of 35000, 56,000 Naval Infantry/Marines including two multi-arm marine brigades and a 56,000 strong naval air arm operating several hundred land-based aircraft and ship-based helicopters.

Indigenous production of its nuclear-powered submarine, the Type-093 has commenced. The Type-094 nuclear powered and nuclear JL-2 missile armed submarine, the new Shan Class submarines, the DF-31 and DF-31A intercontinental ballistic missiles (ICBMS) are being developed. An agreement has been concluded with Russians for 3 Sovereinmny class destroyers and 12 Kilo class submarines.

Strategic Missile Forces

China started its nuclear program in 1955. The first nuclear test was conducted on 16 October 1964. The Second Artillery Corps was formed on 1 July 1966. The Second Artillery Corps (SAC) is the strategic missile forces of the PLA. It controls China's nuclear and conventional strategic missiles. China's total nuclear arsenal size is estimated to be between 100 and 400 nuclear weapons. The SAC has approximately 90,000 to120,000 personnel and six ballistic missile divisions. The six divisions are independently deployed in different military regions and have a total of 15 to 20 missile brigades. It is estimated that China has about 100-160 liquid fuelled ICBMs capable of striking the United States. It has approximately 100 to150 IRBMs capable of striking Russia or Eastern Europe. China also possesses several hundred tactical SRBM with ranges between 300 and 600km. China is reported to have deployed around one thousand M-9 missiles on its eastern coast, targeting Taiwan. As a part of its "counter-India" strategy, China has deployed medium range nuclear ballistic missiles like the DF-21 and DF-21A to cover most of India. Its growing fleet of its nuclear submarines is eventually going to patrol the Indian Ocean. The CIA has said in 2002 that China will quadruple or quintuple its number of long-range nuclear missiles by 2015.

Space Based System

The PLA has deployed a number of space-based systems for military purposes. These include the intelligence satellite systems like the Zi Yan series and the militarily designated Jian Bing series, synthetic aperture satellites (SAR) such as Jian Bing-5, Bei Dou satellite navigation system and secured communication satellites. The PLA has started the development of an anti-ballistic and anti-satellite system in the 1960s, code named Project 640, including ground-based lasers, and anti-satellite missiles. On January 11, 2007 China conducted a successful test of an anti-satellite missile, with an SC-19 class KKV.

Cyber Warfare Capability

Chinese cyber warfare is meant to disable the opponent's communication systems. China has rapidly developed its cyber warfare capability. In the last two years China's military hackers defaced India's Defence Ministry and Bhaba Atomic Research Centre (BARC) Websites. Although no real damage was done, these are precursors. Chinese hackers have also occasionally hacked into Pentagon and White House computer systems. Recently, a cyber-attack, possibly by North Koreans, disabled many computer networks in the US and South Korea for almost one week.

Defence Production Capability

Right from independence in October 1949, the Chinese strongly believed in self-reliance in military equipment. Initially, a considerable amount of Soviet technology was transferred to China. The Soviet technology transfers stopped coming from the mid-1950s onwards. But since 1971, Chinese have been shopping in the international market for weapon systems and spent considerable amount of its money in modernizing its armed forces. Since 1980 China is a major producer and exporter of weapon systems. Some may question the performance of weapon systems that China is selling in the international market. But Pakistan, North Korea, Bangladesh, Sri Lanka and Iran have bought their equipment and are equipping their armies with the same. Chinese equipment saw action in the Iraq-Iran war of the 1990s. The Iranians used the Silkworm missiles from China quite successfully to confront Iraq.

Defence industries in China produce sufficient surplus for China to have become a leading arms supplier in the world. Economic reforms introduced by leader Deng Xiaoping in 1979 resulted in major changes in China's arms industry during the 1980s. The reforms enabled individual government agencies and public institutions, including those within the military, to set up their own commercial companies. As a consequence, numerous sub-units within the military complex began operating profit-making companies involved in arms manufacturing, imports and exports. The largest Chinese arms companies include Norinco or China North Industries Corporation, China Poly Group Corporation, which is one of the largest Chinese arms exporting companies and is operated by PLA's General Staff Department and Xinxing Corporation, which is operated by the PLA General Logistics Department

Chinese defence industries have been assisted by western firms who have provided technological assistance for money. One example is the Z-10 attack helicopter developed by China Helicopter Research and Development Institute. China is buying skills and off the shelf technology and routing them in to military programs.

Chinese arms deals often involve an exchange of weapons for raw materials. In the 1990s, the PLA exported arms to Iran in return for oil. China is the major arms supplier to its allies like Pakistan, Myanmar, Bangladesh and Sri Lanka. China is also a major supplier of arms to Sudan, Liberia, Zimbabwe, Venezuela etc. The exports include small arms and light weapons, artillery guns, tanks, armored personnel carriers, anti tank missiles, fighter aircraft and helicopters. The exports are worth billions of US dollars and help China get political support in these countries.

Summary

The New Border Law which came into force on January 1, 2022 prevents China from giving up any territory that historically was a part of it. So military and diplomatic negotiations between India and China are meaningless. India should either be ready to surrender disputed territories including Arunachal Pradesh or get ready to fight.

It will be seen from above that the Chinese Armed forces are the largest in the world and its air force and navy are the third largest after the US and Russians. With over 2 trillion US dollars as its foreign exchange reserve, it seeks to be the number one military power in the world. It may take fifteen to twenty years to achieve this goal. **But that is not much of a solace to India which is falling behind every year.**

Analysis

India should not be awed by the size of Chinese Armed Forces. What is important is for the Indian military leadership to assess what China can deploy in various sectors of our borders, in what time frame and deploy forces and reserves accordingly. India must deploy adequate early warning and intelligence systems to ensure we are not surprised. Technology and human intelligent must be used. **With the present Chinese focus on Taiwan, it is unlikely that it can deploy any additional troops against India.**

Technological or numerical superiority does not ensure victory in battle. Rome fell to barbarians. Taliban in Afghanistan with no air power or artillery defeated the mighty US and captured enough military equipment to make them a formidable fighting force. Indian armoured units equipped with Second World War vintage Sherman and Centurian tanks defeated Pakistani armoured units equipped with the latest M 47/M 48 American Patton tanks in the battles of Phillora and Asal Uttar during the 1965 Indo-Pak war. More than a hundred Pakistani tanks were destroyed and 30 new tanks were abandoned on the battle field by the Pakistanis. **The will to fight and will to win, particularly of the infantry and armoured forces, is decisive. China has a three-year contract army comprising of only sons.** Its infantry and armour have not been tested in a hot war since 1979, when they were soundly defeated by Vietnam. **Considering that each Chinese soldier is an only son and a contract soldier, the fighting capability of Chinese infantry and armoured units likely to be poor.**

India needs to adopt offensive defence and dominate the no man's land between troops of the two countries deployed at the LAC. The no use of fire arms is ridiculous. It encourages the Chinese to constantly send patrols into Indian territory knowing that no harm will befall them. They must be discouraged from crossing the LAC.

The only way of securing our borders with China permanently is to help Tibetans liberate Tibet. About 500 terrorists have tied down over 100,000 security personnel in Kashmir. Imagine the havoc 10,000 Tibetan freedom fighters could do to the PLA in much more under developed and sparsely populated Tibet.

CHAPTER FOUR

China's Relations with Pakistan

Background

Pakistan became the third non-communist country and the fist Muslim country to recognize Peoples Republic of China in 1950. Diplomatic relation between the two countries was established in 1951. Pakistan became an Islamic Republic in 1956. Just two years later the military took control of the nation. Field Marshal Ayub Khan became president. Ayub took advantage of the cold war and established close relations with the US and the West. Pakistan joined two formal military alliances, the Baghdad Pact (later known as CENTO) which included Iran, Iraq and Turkey to defend the Middle East and the Persian Gulf against the Soviet Union and SEATO which covered South-East Asia. As a result, America provided substantial military aid in the form of small arms, tanks, anti-tank weapons, artillery and fighter aircraft.

Defence cooperation between Pakistan and China began in 1963 when Pakistan ceded a part of Pakistan Occupied Kashmir (POK) in the Karakorum mountains as a part of their border settlement pact of March 3, 1963. Since then, China has emerged as Pakistan's single most trusted and enduring military ally. This cooperation is based on their mutual antagonism towards India. It is also beneficial to both the countries. Pakistan is a major market for Chinese weapons and products. Pakistan does not have a strong domestic industrial, scientific and technological base. China supplies Pakistan with cheap products and technologies. It also provides the required political and moral support to Pakistan at the UN when required. In return Pakistan gives China access to western technologies that arrive in Pakistan. It also gives China vital access to the Arabian Sea.

Pakistan was close to the US to start with. It became a part of treaties sponsored by the US as a part of Cold War. It received military and financial aid from the US. It had played an important role in bridging the communication gap between the PRC and the US by facilitating President Nixon's visit to China in 1972. **The United States stopped military aid to both India and Pakistan during the Indo – Pak War of 1965. This was responsible for an increasing emphasis within Pakistan for self-reliance in defence production. This also pushed Pakistan closer towards China in an attempt to diversify its sources of weapons and other equipment.** Pakistan defied considerable American pressure to seek a strategic relationship with China. China provided diplomatic support to Pakistan in its war with India in 1965 and 1971.

The U.S. under President Nixon supported Pakistan in the 1971 in its war with India. However, **the US suspended all American military assistance and any new economic aid in 1990 under the Pressler Amendment amidst concerns that Pakistan was attempting to develop a nuclear weapon.** Given the support that Pakistan had given the US during the Soviet occupation in Afghanistan, many Pakistanis saw this as a betrayal. This belief was further strengthened as India had developed a nuclear weapon without significant American opposition. Pakistan felt the need to follow suit. Thus, the geopolitical alliance between Pakistan and China has since 1990 branched out into military and economic cooperation.

Cordial relations with China have been a pillar of Pakistan's foreign policy. China strongly supported Pakistan's opposition to Soviet involvement in Afghanistan 1970. Pakistan perceives China as a regional counterweight to India. Pakistan also serves as China's main bridge to the Islamic world.

The Long History of Defence Cooperation

The first formal step towards Sino-Pak defence cooperation was taken soon after 1965 war between India and Pakistan. China provided technical and financial assistance for setting up an ordnance factory at Dhaka, East Pakistan. A number of factories for producing defence equipment were set up with the help of Chinese assistance and expertise.

China provided assistance to Pakistan in setting up facilities for the overhauling of Chinese tanks, and license production of the Chinese Tanks and BMPs. China's weapon production company Norinco has also helped Pakistan in the manufacture of Chinese T-69 and T-85 II MBT and M-113 Armoured Personnel Carriers. **Al-Khalid Main Battle Tank (Pakistan's** own MBT) project began in 1988 at Taxila with Chinese collaboration and was completed in 1992. The 'Al-Khalid' is also called MBT-2000. Primary prototypes produced in China were fielded for trials in August 1991. Production is in progress since 2001. Some of these tanks have been provided to Bangladesh and Sri Lanka.

The F-6 Rebuild Factory was set up as a turnkey project by China and became operational in November 1980. **The Chinese F-6 fighter aircraft became the mainstay of the Pakistan Air Force (PAF) after the American F-86 Sabers were phased out.** China later built overhauling facilities for the F-6 fighter and the Tumansky RD-9B-8II turbojet engines in Pakistan. Later, China also expanded this factory to undertake the overhauling of FT-5, FT-6 and FT-7s Chinese fighter aircraft. **When the F-6s were phased out, the facility was diversified towards maintenance and overhaul of the F-7Ps.The JF-17 Thunder aircraft developed with Chinese assistance is being produced in Pakistan since 2008.**

Pakistan's missile development program was started in the 1986 when Pakistan started assembling the Chinese RBS-70 Mk 1 and Mk 2 air defence missiles systems. Collaboration in the area of longer-range missiles with the Chinese began once Pakistan became involved in financing their M-9 and M-11 missiles programs. General Mirza Aslam Beg is on record for having told the press after a visit to Beijing in 1987 that China's Red Arrow anti-tank missiles were better than US TOW-11. **Chinese help is suspected to be responsible for Pakistan's successful testing in early 1989 of its Hatf II missile with a 300 km range.** The US intelligence agencies have reported that China has transferred about 30 or more of its intermediate range M-11 missiles to Pakistan. Both China and Pakistan have repeatedly denied this report. **China has also provided significant assistance to Pakistan's ballistic missile program in the year 2000 which has put the country on the road to serial production of Short-Range Ballistic Missiles like Shaheen-1 and Haider-1. China continues to provide significant assistance to Pakistan's ballistic missile program and Pakistan is moving toward serial production of solid propellant Short Range Ballistic Missiles.** With the US withdrawal from Afghanistan, Pakistan has adopted a foreign policy which favours China over Washington. Pakistan sees China as a more reliable ally over the long term.

Arms Supplies to Pakistan

China has been the most important supplier of arms to Pakistan since the mid-1960s. Pakistan's military initially depended almost entirely on US arms aid. US supplies of weapon systems like Patton Tanks and Sabre jet fighter encouraged Pakistan to attack India in 1965. This aid was increased during the covert U.S. support of Islamic militants in the Soviet-Afghan War 1980-89. The US sanctions made during the 1965 Indo-Pak war and later for its support to Taliban in Afghanistan has made Pakistan more dependent on arms imports from China. As a result, **China has supplied Pakistan with more than 1,600 main battle tanks, 400 combat aircraft and about 40 naval vessels.** China, in fact, has developed such a stake in supplying arms to Pakistan that it has often flouted its commitment to both the Nuclear Non-Proliferation treaty (NPT) as also the Missile Technology Control Regime (MTCR). Pakistan is China's biggest arms buyer, counting for nearly 50% of Chinese arms exports. Given these realities there is no reason to presume that the China Pakistan military nexus will not increase over time.

Some of the important weapon systems supplied over the years to Pakistan army include about 1000 T-59 MBTs, 600 T-82 MBTs, 100 T-63 light tanks, 100 122mm self-propelled artillery guns. In 2017, Pakistan Army imported Chinese-built Low to Medium Altitude Air Defence System (LOMADS) LY-80 for its air defence system.

The Pakistani air force has been supplied with over 140 F-6 fighters, 140 Q-5 fighters, 100 F-7 fighter bombers and an unspecified number of IL28 bombers. The F-7 are multi role combat aircraft with a range of 850km and can reach most cities in north west India. The delivery of 250 JF17 fighters and 30 J-10 fighters (based on American F 16 design) was discussed during General Tariq Majid's visit to China in January 2009. Pakistan is said to be acquiring the Chengdu C-10 B fighter jet which are said to be equivalent of the US F-16C.

The Pakistani navy has been supplied with 12 Shanghai Class patrol boats, 4 Hainan Class patrol boats, 4 Huchan class and 4 Hegu Class fast attack craft and 2 Romeo class destroyers. China also promised to expedite the delivery of four F-22 frigates. Two of the same were delivered in 2008. China concluded sale of eight conventional submarines worth $5bn in 2015. The Chinese are also helping Pakistan in developing one of its key naval bases at Gwadar, which is strategically located at the mouth of the Strait of Hormuz. The Chinese Navy has access to this port. It gives the Chinese warships and submarines a base to operate from in the Arabian Sea.

China and Pakistan are involved in several projects to enhance military and weaponry systems, which include the joint development of the JF-17 Thunder fighter aircraft, K-8 Karakoram advanced jet trainer and AAWAC systems, Al-Khalid tanks based on the Chinese Type 90 and/or MBT-2000. The Chinese has designed tailor-made advanced weapons for Pakistan.

China-Pakistan Nuclear Cooperation

China helped Pakistan become a nuclear weapons power. China-Pakistan nuclear cooperation began in the early 1980s. It is believed that China assisted Pakistan in developing nuclear weapons prior to it joining the NPT in 1992. **In 1983, US intelligence agencies reported that China had transferred a complete nuclear weapon design to Pakistan, along with enough weapon grade uranium for two nuclear weapons.** China also helped Pakistan operate its Kahuta uranium enrichment plant. In 1986, China concluded a comprehensive nuclear cooperation agreement with Pakistan. China also involved Pakistani scientists in a nuclear test at its Lop Nor test site in 1989. It is believed that China carried out a nuclear test for Pakistan at the same site in 1990. It was because of Chinese assistance that Pakistan could carry out successful nuclear weapons tests within a day of India's nuclear tests on 26 May 1998.

China and Pakistan have cooperated in setting up nuclear power plants in Pakistan. On December 31, 1991, China signed a contract to build the Chashma 300 MW nuclear power reactor for Pakistan. As China pledged to only transfer materials to safeguarded facilities, Pakistan signed an IAEA-safeguards (limited-scope) agreement for the reactor at Chashma. In 1993 China and the International Atomic Energy Agency (IAEA) signed an agreement to apply IAEA safeguards for a Chinese nuclear power plant sold to Pakistan. Pakistan's Chashma Nuclear Power Plant, which is built by Chinese firms, was commissioned in November 1999. China continues providing equipment and technology for the construction of a 40 MW reactor at Khushab. The reactor provides Pakistan with weapon grade plutonium for its weapons program. In March of 2003, China and Pakistan signed an MOU to construct phase 2 of the Chashma facility, a second 300 MW nuclear power plant. The exact progress of the project is not known. A subsidiary of the China National Nuclear Corporation is said to have provided 5,000 custom made ring magnets, which are a key component of the bearings that facilitate the high-speed rotation of centrifuges.

Economic Cooperation

China and Pakistan signed a free trade agreement in 2008. As a direct result, China will open new industries in Pakistan and Pakistan would be offered free trade zones in China. Pakistan and China have agreed to build first ever train routes along the Karakorum Highway. China may be interested in the oil and gas reserves in Baluchistan province of Pakistan. China is ready to make a large investment in Pakistan's chronically weak manufacturing sector. It is also the only worthwhile partner of Pakistan in defence technology and production. The Karakorum Highway linking northern Pakistan to Western China through Pakistan Occupied Kashmir and the Khunjareb Pass was completed in 1978.

China Mobile announced $1 billion of investment in Pakistan's in telecommunication infrastructure in 2011. China Mobile's subsidy Zong is the 3G and 4G network provider in China. China and Pakistan have signed a multi-billion CPEC agreement. The CPEC will connect Pakistan with China and the Central Asian countries with modern highways. It will connect Kashgar in Xinjian Province through Karakoram Pass to Gwadar Port Baluchistan Province of Pakistan. Gwadar Port will serve as the trade nerve centre for China. Most of its trade including oil with Middle East will be done through the port. The port is operated by the China Overseas Port Holding Company, a state-owned Chinese company.

China's bilateral trade volume with Pakistan for 2017 was more than US$ 20 billion. China's exports to Pakistan grew by about 6% to reach $18 billion whereas Pakistan's exports to China fell by about 4% to about $ 2 billion. The trade deficit along with loans taken by Pakistan to survive has it firmly in a Chinese debt trap.

Pakistan's economy is registering a nosedive on major economic indicators. The country's trade deficit stands at 12 billion dollars, which is the highest ever in its 61year old history. With the global financial crisis pushing it to the brink and its strategic relations with the US strained, Pakistan is once again returning to an old trump card, China. Pakistan's Prime Minister, Imran Khan has approached China for help to tide over its financial problems in February 2022. China has promised to help cash strapped Pakistan avert a financial disaster.

Pakistan has no means to earn the foreign exchange required to pay back China. It is somehow surviving with an IMF loan. Pakistan may not admit it but the truth cannot be hidden from the discerning. **The only way it can payback is by giving Gilgit and Baltistan in Pakistani Occupied Kashmir on 99 years lease in the same way as Sri Lanka has given away**

Hambantota.

Diplomatic Cooperation

The US - Pakistan relations improved after terror strikes on the US on September 11, 2001. President Bush considered Pakistan's help in fighting the Taliban as indispensable. President Obama feels the same way and has increase US economic aid three folds. But Pakistan continues to look up to China for most of its military and nuclear development requirements. The strategic alliance between China and Pakistan is designed to denying India the predominant power status in the South Asia. China supported Pakistan's stand at the UN that the evidence submitted by India, against Jaish e Mohammad chief, Hafeez Saeed regarding his involvement in terrorist strike in Mumbai on 26/11/2009, was not adequate to prosecute him in a court of law. In 2005, China was instrumental in Pakistan getting the status of an observer at the Shanghai Cooperation Organization. India enjoys the same status. More recently, Pakistan played a key role in China attaining a similar status with the South Asian Association for Regional Cooperation (SAARC).

Summary

China has long been one of Pakistan's closest regional partners, with Beijing looking to Islamabad as a counterbalance to India. Pakistanis has little faith in the reliability of relations with Washington. With Afghan War lost and Taliban in power, the US has little to gain from providing military and economic aid to Pakistan. China is the only country in the world that has helped Pakistan set up a nuclear power reactor and is open to Pakistani requests for more reactors. China has also made a visible contribution to Pakistan's progress in several civil and defence related sectors.

China seeks Pakistan's help in neutralizing Islamic terrorists in its Xingjiang Province. It also seeks and gets support for destroying Uighur culture. Pakistan has helped China by locating and destroying scores of Uighur separatists from Xinjiang Province in a training camp in the Gilgit area of POK. The separatists were handed over to the Chinese who promptly executed them. Diplomatic cooperation is also beneficial to China. Chinese presence at Gwadar would help Chinese to keep track of US naval ships in the Gulf. Pakistan is also the geopolitical hub for bringing China, the Gulf including Iran and Africa into a thriving economic interaction.

In spite of its close relations with Pakistan, China has never militarily intervened into the Indo- Pak wars of 1965 and 1971. It is possible that China did not consider itself strong enough to intervene in 1965. Further, in 1965, Pakistan was much closer to US than China. In 1971, India waited till December to start and the privileges they enjoy. However, things have changed. China today is a far greater military and economic power than what it was in 1971. Military infrastructure in Yunnan Province of China is well developed. Myanmar is now firmly in Chinese camp. **So, there is no guarantee that it will not support Pakistan in the future.**

Analysis

Despite the Chinese desire for stronger ties with Pakistan there are two main hurdles. The first major hurdle in this regard is lack of security in Pakistan. Ordinary Pakistanis do not like Chinese presence. A number of Chinese engineers working in the port have been abducted and killed by Baluch separatists forcing some Chinese companies working in the project to leave. There have been a lot of protests by the local population against the presence of Chinese nationals in Baluchistan and Gilgit – Baltistan **They second hurdle is the rise of Islamic fundamentalism in Pakistan.** Presence of ISI Khurasan in Afghanistan and organizations like Pakistani Taliban are dire ct threats to the security of Xinjiang Province which has a substantial Muslim population.

Pakistan has a pathological hatred for India and always demands that the US and the West treat it and India as equals. **It is possible that China will take advantage of this hatred and try to cut India to size at an appropriate time.** China has maintained that Kashmir is disputed territory. It has opposed India's reorganization of the State of Jammu and Kashmir.

The best way to weaken Pakistan further is to sever the China Pakistan Economic Corridor. That is only possible if Tibet is liberated.

CHAPTER FIVE

China's Relations with Bangladesh

Background

To start with, China's relations with Bangladesh were dictated by its friendly relations with Pakistan. It was against secession of East Pakistan and the struggle for independence launched by the people of Bangladesh. **China supported Pakistan against the Mukti Bahini during the Bangladesh Liberation War of 1971.** However, the support to Pakistan was restricted to political and moral support. China could not intervene militarily into the conflict as the operations started in December when the passes on the LAC were snowbound. **In 1972, China exercised its veto power as a permanent member of the UN Security Council to block Bangladesh's entry into the UN.** Bangladesh under Sheikh Mujibur Rehman had aligned itself with India and the Soviet Union, both of whom had strained relations with Pakistan and China. **Following the assassination of Mujibur and overthrow of the Awami League government, the equation changed. Pakistan warmed towards Bangladesh after the overthrow of Mujibur Rahaman and diplomatic relations were established between the two countries in 1975-76.** Pakistan's allies such as Saudi Arabia and China followed suit. **A preliminary agreement between China and Bangladesh to establish diplomatic and economic relations was signed in late 1975 and duly ratified in 1976.** The then president of Bangladesh, Ziaur Rahaman, made an official visit to China in 1977. By the mid-1980s, China had forged close commercial and cultural ties with Bangladesh and also supplied it with military aid and equipment. **In 2002, the Chinese Premier Wen Jiabao made an official visit to Bangladesh and both countries declared 2005 as the "Bangladesh-China Friendship Year."**

1975 - 2008

China did not accord diplomatic recognition to Bangladesh till 1975 when Pakistan did the same. Initially China's relations with Bangladesh were being determined by Pakistan's foreign policy considerations. However, political and strategic realities soon took over and China made serious attempts to wean over Bangladesh from India's influence. Bangladesh became a part of the Chinese game plan to encircle India. Bangladesh thus became a major recipient of Chinese arms. China has assured Bangladesh of enhanced military and economic assistance. Bangladesh on its part endorsed the one China policy of Beijing and considered the recent incidents in Tibet as an internal matter of China.

In 2006, Dhaka emerged as one of the prime buyers of weapons made in China. China sold 65 large calibre artillery systems, 16 combat aircraft and 114 missiles and related equipment to Bangladesh in 2005 besides small arms and 82 mm mortars. In 2008 Bangladesh set up a missile launch pad near the Chittagong Port with assistance from China. Bangladesh performed its maiden missile test on May 12, 2008 with active participation of Chinese experts. It successfully test-fired a ship based anti-ship cruise missile C-802 A with a strike range of 120 km from a frigate near Kutubdia Island in the Bay of Bengal. The frigate was a 1500-ton Chinese built Jianghu class warship commissioned into the Bangladesh Navy and the C-802A missile, according to experts, is a modified version of Chinese Ying Ji missile.

Bangladesh-China Defence Co-operation

A Defence Co-operation Agreement was signed between Bangladesh and China during the visit of Bangladesh Prime Minister, Begum Khaleda Zia to China in 2002. The new agreement was to help institutionalize the existing accords in defence sector and to consolidate the existing piecemeal agreements to enhance cooperation in training, maintenance and some areas in production that had existed since the early eighties. The purpose of Defence Cooperation Agreement was to meet present day up gradation and modernization needs of Bangladesh's defence forces. It was claimed that this defence umbrella agreement was not directed against any country and would not affect Bangladesh's relations with India. **The major significance of the Defence Cooperation Agreement is that it is the first such agreement ever signed by Bangladesh in its history.**

The agreement also helps Pakistan's strategic designs against India because Bangladesh's enhanced military profile with Chinese aid would divert some of India's strategic military assets from the West to the East and lower the pressure on Pakistan. **Rising Islamic fundamentalism in Bangladesh makes it easier to use Bangladesh territory for intensifying Pakistan's proxy war on India's Eastern peripheries.**

China's strategic interests are also served by the Bangladesh-China Defence Cooperation Agreement. The agreement could more aptly be termed as "Bangladesh-China Treaty of Friendship and Strategic Cooperation" with similar intent as the Indo-Soviet Treaty of Friendship and Cooperation of 1971. As a result of the Agreement, China gets a strategic toe hold on India's Eastern flank in Bangladesh. China's strategic encirclement of India is enhanced through the treaty. **China could start developing the Chittagong Naval Base on the lines of Gwadar in Pakistan** and in return get naval bases facility in Bangladesh.

2008 to Present

Awami League returned to power in the 2008 general election. Sheikh Hasina became the Prime Minister.

The 2014 General election was boycotted by BNP and other opposition parties. Awami League won a landslide victory. The 2018 General election was marred by allegations of vote rigging. Awami League again won a landslide victory. **Anti-India trend has somewhat reduced with the pro India Awami League coming to power. But this could be a temporary phase. As Sun Tzu said, one should not rely on intentions of a nation but on its military capability. Intentions can change with change of government. But it takes a lot of time and money to build a viable deterrence.** Chinese may be back in Bangladesh.

Summary

Bangladesh was created in December 1971 when India defeated the Pakistan Army in erstwhile East Pakistan and handed over power to Sheikh Mujibur Rehman, its first Prime Minister. **In spite this, Bangladesh has been unfriendly to India during most of its 41 years of independence.** As Bangladesh had been a part of Pakistan and has a predominantly Muslim population, it draws its political and strategic ideologies from Pakistan and Saudi Arabia. Like Pakistan, Bangladesh's politics get defined in the context of anti-India stances.

Like Pakistan, Bangladesh had come under growing influence of Islamic fundamentalists. During the past government of Begum Khaleda Zia, the Jamaat group was part of the ruling coalition. **Bangladesh shares a long and porous 3901 kms border with India.** This has enabled more than 2 million Bangladeshi nationals to move into India as illegal immigrants. Bangladesh offers Pakistan a fertile ground for basing its proxy war apparatus to strategically weaken India on its East and North Eastern peripheries. This arises from common religious links and shared heritage of its intelligence and military establishments with those of Pakistan. **Like the Pakistan Army, the Bangladesh Army has over thrown civilian governments and ruled the country under martial law.**

Analysis

The Pakistan-China strategic nexus in South Asia can come into play in Bangladesh. The Bangladesh-China Defence Cooperation is a result of this geopolitical environment. **The current Awami League government may be more favourably disposed towards India. But governments and policies of nations keep changing.** The growing military cooperation between China and Bangladesh including the Bangladesh-China Defence Cooperation Agreement has serious strategic and tactical implications for India.

The threat is best reduced by reducing China's influence. That in turn is best achieved by getting China involved in fighting insurgencies in Tibet and Xinjian, India must help Tibetans liberate Tibet.

CHAPTER SIX

China's Relationship with Sri Lanka

Background

Sri Lanka became independent of British rule as a dominion in 1948. Sri Lanka's relations with India were very cordial to start with. **Sri Lanka Government recognized Peoples Republic of China in 1950. China and Sri Lanka established diplomatic relations in 1957. Premier Zhou Enlai visited Sri Lanka twice in 1957 and 1964.** Sri Lanka Prime Minister Mrs Bandaranaike visited China respectively in 1961 and 1972. The two countries have maintained cordial relations and exchanged visits of dignitaries ever since. The Sri Lanka Government has always pursued a friendly policy toward China and strongly supported China on the Taiwan and Tibet questions and human rights issue. The two countries share consensus on many major international issues and enjoy sound cooperation between them.

The Civil War

The Sinhalese majority's mounting resentment at the Tamil minority's monopoly on political and economic power led to conflict. In July 1983 communal riots took place all over Sri Lanka due to the ambush and killing of 13 Sri Lankan Army soldiers by the Tamil Tigers. The Tamil community faced a backlash from Sinhalese rioters. Homes and shops of Tamils were burned and Tamils were assaulted. During these riots the government did nothing to control the mob. Around 18,000 Tamil homes and 5,000 shops were destroyed. Over 150,000 Tamils left the country creating a Tamil Diaspora in Canada, UK, Australia and other western countries. Tamil rebel groups, the strongest of which were the Liberation Tigers of Tamil Elam, or LTTE, began a civil war to fight for a separate Tamil nation or "Elam". **Relations between Sri Lanka and India soured somewhat with the rise** of the ethnic conflict between the Sinhalese and the Tamil people as Sri Lanka believed that the Tamils were being aided by India in their search for "Elam".

In 1987, there was an army offensive in the Jaffana peninsular which led to large scale human rights abuses against the Tamil population. India started getting deeply involved in the ethnic conflict. A naval convoy with humanitarian aid sent by India was stopped in Sri Lankan waters by the Sri Lankan Navy. The Indian Air Force retaliated with an air drop of supplies onto the Jaffna peninsula. The Sri Lankan government organized street protests against India. Prime Minister Mr. Jayawardene declared that he would defend the country's independence to the last bullet. Indo-Sri Lankan relations began to deteriorate. **However, the display of Indian military power through the air drop caused Mr. Jayawardene to reconsider his position.** He accepted the offer of Indian Prime Minister Rajiv Gandhi of a Peace Accord. Rajiv Gandhi sent a Peace Keeping Force (IPKF) into Sri Lanka. The move was deeply unpopular with the Sinhalese and initially popular with the Tamils. **But IPKF's attempts to restrain the LTTE led to an outbreak of hostilities between the Tamil Tigers and the IPKF. This is known as Eelam War II. Indo-Sri Lankan relations reached its nadir.**

In 1989 Mr. Jayewardene was succeeded by Mr. Premadasa as president of Sri Lanka. Premadasa asked for the Indian troops to be withdrawn. This was done by Indian Prime Minister Mr. V P Singh. Mr. Rajeev Gandhi was assassinated by a Tamil Tiger suicide bomber in 1991. This led to LTTE being declared a terrorist organization by the Indian government and banned. Relations between India and Sri Lanka began to improve.

President Premadasa was assassinated by a Tamil Tiger suicide bomber in 1992. Mrs Kumaratunga was elected President in August 1994. A ceasefire Sri Lankan Army and LTTE followed. But it did not last long. The Tamil Tigers broke the ceasefire and started the Elam War III. The Sri Lankan military was unable to defeat the separatists and the government was opposed to negotiations. By 2000 an estimated 65,000 people, mostly civilians had been killed in the conflict. Mr. Wickremasinghe became Prime Minister in December 2001and another cease fire began. In March 2004, the President dismissed Mr. Wickremesinghe and called fresh elections. **Mr. Mahinda Rajapakshe, the present president of Sri Lanka,** thus came to power. He **decided on a military solution to the ethnic problem.** He left no stone unturned to strengthen the armed forces and launched an all-out offensive against the LTTE in July 2006. Thus, Elam War IV started.

After about three years of bitter fighting, the Sri Lankan government declared total victory on May 18, 2009. The Sri Lankan military, thus, effectively concluded its 26 year operation against the LTTE. Sri Lankan Defence Secretary confirmed that 6,261 personnel of the Sri Lankan Armed Forces had lost their lives and 29,551 were wounded during Elam War IV. Approximately 22,000 LTTE cadres had died during this time. Over 60,000 civilians also died and about 1.5 million Tamils have been rendered homeless.

The Dragon Enters

Once President Rajapakshe had decided to impose a military solution to the Tamil Elam issue, he had to find a way to strengthen the armed forces and find a way to economically sustain the conflict. India and the West were not willing to support a military solution. So Rajapakshe turned to China and its ally, Pakistan. The Chinese Government seized the opportunity with both hands and provided the Sri Lankan Government arms, ammunitions, tanks, fighter planes and all military and economic assistance necessary to win the war. China has promised continued support of the Chinese government for Sri Lanka's sovereignty, territorial integrity and President Mahinda Rajapaksa's efforts to bring about a solution to the ethnic conflict and achieve ethnic solidarity in the country through military action. This support has enabled Sri Lanka's government to jettison a five-year cease-fire in 2008 and go for an all-out military action against the LTTE. Sri Lankan government ignores India's concerns about the Sri Lankan Tamils and also ignores complaints from US and European Union about human rights violations in the war. The government has lost defence aid from the United States. But the loss has been more than made up by military aid from China and Pakistan.

In exchange for Chinese support, the Sri Lankan Government agreed to the establishment of a Chinese naval base to be built on the Sri Lankan coast. China has thus been able to strengthen its position in the geopolitical struggle for power over the energy trade routes along the Indian ocean.

Military Co-operation

China declared support for Sri Lankan Government in its battle against the LTTE. China came to Colombo's rescue after US stopped aid to Sri Lanka because of its human rights violations. Sri Lanka signed a US$ 37.6 million classified arms deal with Chinese defence manufacturers in April 2007, to supply small arms, ammunition and equipment for its army and navy. Beijing has also roped in its ally Pakistan into providing arms to Sri Lanka. China sold huge quantities of arms to Sri Lanka in 2008 and boosted annual aid from $ 200 million in 2007 to $ 1 billion in 2008. China is now the largest donor to Sri Lanka. Its Jian 7 fighter jets and anti-aircraft guns, JY 11-3D air surveillance radars played a key role in Sri Lanka's successes against the LTTE. Pakistan has trained the Sri Lankan air force in ground attacks and precision bombing. (Times News Network April 27, 2009). The phenomenal increase in the Sri Lankan Army that was required to defeat LTTE was possible through Chinese arms aid and purchase of Chinese equipment. Most of the Army is equipped with Chinese equipment. Some of the equipment available with the Sri Lankan army include T55, Type 59, Type 63, BMP1, BMP2, BMP3, Nornico Type 89, Type 93, BTR 80 and BTR 152 armoured personnel carriers, 122mm, 130mm and 152mm howitzers, RM70 and BM21 multi-barrel rocket launchers, 60mm, 82mm and 120mm mortars and Bakhtar Sikha anti-tank missiles. In October 2016, the Chinese government announced it would offer military aid to Sri Lanka to help them purchase Chinese made military equipment. China also helped the Sri Lanka Air Force set up the Aircraft Overhaul Wing and provided Chinese specialists who assisted and guided the SLAF.

Economic Relations

China is increasing the volume of its investments in Sri Lanka. **When the US ended military aid in 2007 over Sri Lanka's human-rights concerns, China provided Sri Lanka $1bn to become the island's biggest donor, giving tens of millions of dollars' worth of military equipment.** Thus, Chinese assistance grew fivefold surpassing Japan, formerly Sri Lanka's largest economic supporter. China has recently started explorations for oil in Sri Lanka. It provided financial and technical support for the construction of a new port and bunker facilities at Hambantota. The Hambantota Bunkering system and Tank Farm Project was undertaken by the Chinese government subsequent to a visit of Chinese Premier Wen Jiabao to Sri Lanka from April 2005. It will cost about $300 million. The project has already begun. China is also funding a coal powered power plant that will generate 20 giga watts by the year 2020. A sum of Rs. 1.5 billion (US $ 15m), would be invested by the Chinese Harbour Engineering Company for the re-constructing six fisheries harbours out of the 10 destroyed by the tsunami. This would be completed within a period of 18 months. The Chinese entrepreneurs would also get involved in the Puttalam Coal Power, the Colombo – Katunayake Expressway, Colombo – Katunayake Airport

Rail link, the Phosphate Mining and NPK Compound Fertilizer Project and the Kotte Sewerage System Project. China has given loans to Sri Lanka for infrastructure investments including the Hambantota Port, Hambantota International Airport and the ambitious Colombo Port City project which the Chinese President Xi Jinping launched in 2014.

The Sri Lankan government is facing economic problems and inflation is expected to reach double digits. The Western nations and UN are unhappy with Sri Lanka's human rights record. They want war crimes investigations to be carried out. Sri Lankan government has refused to do so. Its defiance of the West caused Sri Lanka to lose trade preferences with the European Union and the US. Covid and interfaith violence has considerably reduced inflow of foreign tourists and foreign exchange. There is also a huge debt repayment to China. Sri Lanka is finding it difficult to find foreign exchange to buy oil.

Chinese engineering companies who have been contracted for projects in Sri Lanka have also brought in migrant workers from China. They are working on major infrastructure projects. The influx of Chinese workers has boosted some local economies.

Hambantota Port

Hambantota port was financed through Chinese loans, and built by a Chinese company. Unable to repay, the two countries have recently come to a deal with Sri Lanka selling an 80% stake via a 99-year lease in the port to a Chinese company. The Sri Lankan Foreign Minister Ravi Karunanayake called the port an unaffordable investment that doesn't bring any economic returns. China is also building a 15000-acre industrial zone near Hambantota port, in which it will have a major stake and will also be ceded to China for 99 years. **Both of these projects have led to fears among the local population that the area will become a "Chinese colony". This has led to violent protests by locals including Buddhist monks who stand to lose their lands against the port and the industrial zone.** It is believed that the Chinese see their stake in the Hambantota port project not only as a method to gain favour with the Sri Lankan government but also as a way to establish a strategic Chinese naval presence on the primary sea trade route that lies just six nautical miles away. **Sri Lanka is now a major country home to the "String of Pearls" naval bases, which is a part of the Chinese strategic initiative to strengthen their naval presence in the Indian Ocean.**

China-Sri Lankan Tamil Relations

China helped the Sri Lankan Government to defeat the Tamils. In return they have the strategic port of Hambantota. It also has Sri Lanka securely in a debt trap and is acquiring parts of Sri Lanka on 99 years lease. Sri Lanka has nothing more to offer.

China is now trying to befriend the Sri Lankan Tamils. They have a consulate at Jaffna. Recently, Chinese diplomats in Tamil "Lungis" (traditional dhoti dress worn by Tamil men during social and religious functions) along with their wives carried out a photo operation at a Tamil Hindu temple and displayed their solidarity with the Tamils of Sri Lanka. **It is possible that they will pressurise the Sri Lankan Government to give autonomy to the Tamil majority regions in the northern and eastern Sri Lanka. Then they could try to use the Sri Lankan Tamils to encourage separatism in Tamil Nadu Province of India.**

Sri Lanka is today a bankrupt nation. It is unable to repay its loans to China and other lenders. Its economy has collapsed. Its foreign exchange reserve is almost nil. India has extended a credit line for purchase of food, medicine and petroleum products. But that has not prevented Sri Lanka from letting a Chinese spy ship from docking at Hambantota in spite of Indian objections.

Summary

China helped Sri Lankan Government defeat the LTTE in the civil war by providing military and economic aid. It also gave a lot of economic aid for developing infrastructure. Now it has Sri Lanka in a debt trap. It has secured the Hambantota Port and area near Colombo on 99 years lease. Chinese companies and their Chinese labour are in Sri Lanka to stay for ever.

Lately, China has started to improve relation with the Tamils of Sri Lanka. Their only motive could be to use Sri Lankan Tamils to start a separatist movement in Tamil Nadu.

Analysis

Cordial relations between India and Sri Lanka are impossible unless Sri Lanka is able to successfully bridge the communal divide and move away from Chinese influence. The latter is impossible in near term.

The Chinese want to have dominating influence in Sri Lanka due to the island's strategic location near important shipping routes in the Indian Ocean. China sees these sea lanes as vital because its energy supplies pass through the Indian Ocean region.

Chinese presence in Sri Lanka furthers its strategy of containing Indian influence. China will utilize economic tools such as aid, trade and infrastructural development as well as enhanced military cooperation to retain their control over Sri Lanka. **China will also befriend Sri Lankan Tamils in the hope of fomenting trouble in Tamil Nadu.**

A hostile Sri Lanka aided by Chinese Navy will make it difficult for the Indian Navy to move its naval assets from the Bay of Bengal to the Arabian Sea and vice versa at war time.

India provided Sri Lanka with over $4 billion worth of food, fuel and medicines during their recent economic collapse. But it could not persuade Sri Lanka not to allow a Chinese spy ship dock at Hambantota. Indian cannot stop Sri Lanka from becoming a Chinese alley.

The only option for India is to weaken China. The best way to do that is to help Tibetans liberate Tibet.

CHAPTER SEVEN

China's Relations with Myanmar

Background

Myanmar gained independence on January 4, 1948. The early years of Myanmar's independence were marked by insurgencies by communist groups and ethnic tribes. Myanmar initially strove to be non-aligned in world affairs. **It was one of the first countries in the world to recognize the Peoples Republic of China.** By 1958, the country was beginning to fall apart politically due to a split in the ruling party. The military feared that communists would come to power. **Mr. U Nu, the first prime minister, invited Army Chief General Ne Win to take over the country.** Communist sympathizers were purged. Ne Win's caretaker government successfully stabilized the situation. New general elections were held in 1960. U Nu's Union Party returned with a large majority.

1962–1988

In March 1962, the army under General Ne Win staged a coup and declared Myanmar a socialist state. A number of protests followed the coup but they were ruthlessly suppressed by the military. **All opposition parties were banned in 1964.**

The Kachin Independence Organization (KIO) started an insurgency in 1961 when Prime Minister U Nu declared Buddhism as the state religion. The Shan State Army also launched a rebellion in 1964 because of the 1962 military coup. **Ne Win isolated the country from contact with the rest of the world. A one-party system was established.** Commerce and industry were nationalized across the board. In April 1972, General Ne Win and the rest of the Revolutionary Council retired from the military but continued to run the country. A new constitution was promulgated in January 1974 that resulted in the creation of a People's Assembly that held supreme legislative, executive, and judicial authority. Ne Win became the president of the new government.

In 1978, a military operation was conducted against the Rohingiya Muslims in Arakan region bordering Bangladesh. This resulted in about 250,000 refugees fleeing to neighbouring Bangladesh.

1988- 2008

1980s saw widespread protests and demonstrations throughout the country. The military responded by firing on the crowds, alleging Communist infiltration. Violence, chaos and anarchy reigned. **The armed forces staged another coup on September 18, 1988 to restore order. The military killed thousands, abolished the 1974 Constitution and imposed martial law.**

The military government announced a change of name for the country from Burma to Myanmar in 1989. It also continued the economic reforms started by the old regime and called for a Constituent Assembly to revise the 1974 Constitution. **This led to multi-party elections in May 1990 in which the National League for Democracy (NLD) won a landslide victory. The military government, however, did not let the assembly convene. It placed the leader of the NLD, Aung San Suu Kyi under house arrest.** Burma came under increasing international pressure to convene the elected assembly, particularly after Aung San Suu Kyi was awarded the Nobel Peace Prize in 1991.

The Military Junta finally allowed a national convention to meet in 1993 to review the constitution but insisted that the assembly preserve a major role for the military in any future government. The NLD was not ready to accept the condition and walked out. The government reconvened the National Convention in 1995 in an attempt to rewrite the Constitution. The Military Junta relaxed some of the restrictions on Aung San Suu Kyi's house arrest and finally released her in 1995. She was forbidden to leave Yangon. However, major pro-democracy organizations and parties, including the NLD, were barred from participating. The military allowed only selected smaller parties to participate. But a new constitution could not be agreed upon. The assembly was finally dismissed in March 1996 without producing a constitution.

The military mounted two major crackdowns on the NLD in 1996 and 1997. Continuing reports of human rights violations in Burma led the US to intensify sanctions in 1997. The European Union followed suit in 2000. The military placed Aung San Suu Kyi under house arrest again. She remains under house arrest even today. The government also carried out another large-scale crackdown on the NLD, arrested many of its leaders and closed down most of its offices. The capital city was relocated from Yangon to Naypyidaw in January 2006.

In 2007, the Military Junta removed fuel subsidies which caused the price of diesel and petrol to suddenly rise as much as 100%. This led to large scale protests. The protest demonstrations were dealt with quickly and harshly by the Military junta. Hundreds of protesters arrested and detained. Buddhist monks took part in the protests and were brutally suppressed. On 7 February 2008, the Junta announced that a referendum for the Constitution would be held by 2010 and elections would follow. The referendum was held on May 10, 2008 and elections followed. The military backed USDP party was declared winner and a nominal civilian government was formed under retired General Thein Sein. **Next general election was held in 2015 and was won by Aung San Suu Kyi's NLD Party. The Military Junta was dissolved and a nominally civilian government was installed. Aung San Suu Kyi and other political prisoners were released. Civilian government lasted till 2020. Aung San Suu Kyi's party won a clear majority in both houses. The Myanmar Military was not happy and again seized power in a military coup in Feb 2021.** The coup was widely condemned internally and externally. There were widespread protests which were ruthlessly put down. Aung San Suu Kyi was arrested and charged with various crimes. The coup was immediately condemned by the UN, US and EU. However, some countries including India, China and Russia refrained from criticizing the coup. One year has passed. Military rule continues. Thousands of Burmese nations have been killed. Opponents of the coup have formed a government in exile in the ethnic states in northern Myanmar. Armed and peaceful protests are going on. The Junta has executed four opposition leaders by firing squad. Aung San Suu Kyi has been put in prison for more than six years on corruption charges.

China Myanmar Relations

Burma was the first non-Communist country to recognize the Communist-led People's Republic of China after its foundation in 1949. Burma and the People's Republic of China formally established diplomatic relations on June 8, 1950. **China and Burma signed a treaty of friendship and mutual non-aggression and promulgated a Joint Declaration on June 29, 1954.** Beijing had always identified Burma as vital to the well-being to its impoverished provinces in the South-West, Yunnan, Sichuan and Guizhou.

The relations between the two countries turned hostile in the sixties. The Communist Party of Burma (CPB) had fled to China in face of persecution by the military and had received support at the hands of the Communist government in China. There were anti-Chinese riots in 1967 and the Chinese communities were expelled from Burma.

Relations began to improve significantly in the 1970s. Under the rule of Deng Xiaoping, China reduced support for the CPB. In 1988, the Military Junta under the title of "State Peace and Development Council (SDPC)" assumed power and carried out violent repression against pro-democracy agitators. This resulted in growing international condemnation and pressure. **The Military Junta found it necessary to cultivate a strong relationship with China to survive. China signed a major trade agreement with Burma, legalized cross-border trade and began supplying large quantities of military aid.** Thus, China's influence grew rapidly after the international community abandoned Burma. China and Russia have vetoed an UN Security Council resolution designed to punish Burma and may do so in the future.

At the outset of the twenty first century, the overriding goal of the Burmese Military Junta is the survival of its regime. Close and cordial relations with China are a key element of the strategy. As such, the two countries regularly exchange high-level visits. Domestic developments in Myanmar in 2003 and 2004 helped to further strengthen Sino-Myanmar relations. **Following the attacks on Aung San Suu Kyi's entourage by pro-SPDC militias on May 30, 2003, the United States, EU and Japan tightened sanctions against Burma. This has increased Myanmar's reliance on China for economic sustenance.**

The 2021 military coup has strained the relations between the two countries. The Burmese people view China as a supporter of the Military Junta. Many Chinese owned factories and businesses have been torched and damaged during the disturbances that followed the coup,

Economic Relations

Myanmar has very strong economic relations with China. It would not be wrong to say that in the regime of sanctions by US and the European Union, its economic survival depends on Chinese economic support. China has provided soft loans to the military regime as well as economic aid and investments for the construction of dams, bridges, roads, ports and industrial projects. To exploit the river and road networks in Myanmar, China has entered into a long-term agreement with Myanmar.

China is building new roads linking Myanmar with the South-West provinces, clearing the Irrawaddy River for bigger barges and modernizing some of the ports and shipyards of Myanmar. China extensively financed the construction of strategic roads along the Irrawaddy River trade route linking China's Yunan province to the Bay of Bengal.

Myanmar is an important element in China's quest for energy security. It has received the rights to develop and exploit natural gas reserves in the Arakan region. Chinese firms have been involved in the construction of oil and gas pipelines stretching 2,380 km from Burma's Arakan coast to China's Yunnan Province. Petro China is in the process of building a major gas pipeline from the A-1 Shwe oil field, off the coast of Myanmar, to Yunnan, accessing and exploiting an estimated 2.88 to 3.56 trillion cubic feet of natural gas (Refer Map No: 5). A proposed Sino-Myanmar oil pipeline off the western coast of Burma may permit China to import oil from the Middle East bypassing the Straits of Malacca.

Beijing continues to dole out soft loans to the Myanmar government. For instance, in 2003 China helped stabilize the economy after a banking crisis with $200 million in preferential loans and partial debt relief on earlier loans (Financial Times, January 17, 2003). China has maintained its position as Myanmar's top trade and investment partner. In 2005, bilateral trade hit $1.21 billion, much of it in China's favour; China exported $935 million worth of goods to Burma, but only imported $274 million (People's Daily, July 31, 2006). Bilateral trade between China and Burma exceeded $1.4 billion in 2008.

Military Relations

China has extensive strategic and military cooperation with Myanmar. It is the most important supplier of military aid to Myanmar's Military Junta since its takeover of the power in 1988 and has supplied more than $ 3 billion worth of arms since 1989. China has supplied Myanmar with jet fighters, armoured vehicles and naval vessels. It has trained Burmese army, navy and air force personnel. In return, China has been granted access to Burma's ports and naval installations. This has enabled China to increase its strategic influence in the Bay of Bengal and the Indian Ocean. **China has developed a deep-water port at Kyaukpvu in the Bay of Bengal. It has also built a jetty, naval facilities and installed reconnaissance and electronic intelligence systems on the Great Coco Island which is located only 18 km from India's Andaman and Nicobar Islands.** This base gives China the capabilities to monitor India's military activities in the Bay of Bengal, including missile tests. **China is assisting in constructing a naval base at Sittwe, a strategically important sea port. China is also helping Myanmar in modernizing its naval bases at Hanggyi, Akyab and Mergui. Beijing has also funded road construction linking Yangon and Sittwe, providing the shortest route to the Indian Ocean from southern China.**

Myanmar's Relations with India

In recent years, Myanmar has shown an willingness to develop strategic and commercial relations with India. **Once New Delhi committed itself to a policy of remaining silent on the political situation in Myanmar, relations with the SPDC improved rapidly.** The two countries have exchanged high-level visits, including a visit by Indian President A.P.J Abdul Kalam in March 2006. India has supplied the Myanmar Army with tanks, artillery and helicopters. **The two countries' armed forces have conducted coordinated military operations against Indian insurgents.** India has built a highway connecting Manipur with Myanmar's road system. New Delhi is trying to get into exploiting Myanmar's energy resources. Myanmar's trade and military cooperation with India has increased.

Since 2000, Myanmar has also allowed itself to be courted by Russia. Enhanced relations with Moscow have provided the SPDC with several benefits, including an alternative source of arms. Moscow has agreed to provide Myanmar with MiG-29 fighters and air defence systems and invest in the country's energy sector. Russian interest in Burma was demonstrated in January 2007 when Russia vetoed a US proposal for sanctions against Myanmar at the UN Security Council.

Summary

Myanmar is firmly in the Chinese camp. The military junta ruling Myanmar cannot survive without Chinese assistance.

Analysis

As long as the Military Junta (SDPC) remains in power, Beijing will retain its position as Myanmar's primary patron. China's veto power at the UN and financial clout makes it a far more valuable ally than India.

Burma's dependence on China would only increase if Myanmar's relations with ASEAN became more strained and Burma's membership were suspended or forfeited.

If China uses northern Myanmar to attack India as it did in 1962, it is unlikely that the Military Junta will do anything to stop it. The best way to eliminate this danger is to weaken China. The best way to do that is to

help Tibetan freedom fighters liberate Tibet.

CHAPTER EIGHT

China's Relations with Nepal

Background

Nepal became a tributary state of the Chinese Qing Dynasty after being defeated in the Sino-Nepalese War of 1792. But waves of rebellions like the Taiping Rebellion affected China in 1850s and made it impossible for the Dynasty to enforce its writ on Nepal and Tibet. The Nepalese Prime Minister, Jang Bahadur Rana seized the opportunity to declare independence and press for Nepalese objectives in Tibet without the threat of Chinese interference. He declared war on Tibet in March 1855. On April 3, the Nepalese Army defeated the Tibetan army was defeated in the battle for Dzongka. Negotiations for a cease-fire began. Nepal was unable to press its demands with another campaign since its treasury had been exhausted by the costs of the invasion and occupation of the Tibetan country. Tibetan troops now took the offensive. The Nepalese lost 700 men and the survivors fled to the border. Nepal sent reinforcements and recaptured Kuti which he burned before retreating to Listi, back in Nepal. Negotiation resumed after military operations stalled. The Treaty signed at Thapathali ended the war. The Tibetans agreed to pay an annual subsidy of ten thousand rupees to the Nepal Durbar and to allow a Nepalese trading station and agency to be established at Lhasa. Tibet paid lump sum of Rs. 50,001 as first instalment, but refused to pay the following year which caused war between two nations to continue.

Modern Nepal was created when Prithvi Narayan Shah unified the country under his rule and established the Shah Dynasty. Between 1788 and 1791, Nepal invaded Tibet and plundered the Tashilhunpo Monastery at Sighaste. The Chinese responded by dispatching a large army that defeated the Nepalese army. **Nepal and the British in India fought the Anglo-Nepalese War from 1814 to 1816. Nepal was soundly defeated and had to sign the Treaty of Sugauli in 1816. Nepal ceded the territories of Terrai**

and Sikkim to the British. In exchange Nepal was not annexed by the British. Terrai became a part of India. Sikkim was later annexed by India.

In 1846, a military leader of Indian ancestry overthrew the Shah Dynasty and established the Rana Dynasty of hereditary prime ministers. The Shah Dynasty remained titular rulers. The Ranas were staunchly pro-British and assisted the British during the Sepoy Mutiny of 1857.

The Indian struggle for independence inspired the Nepalese people to demand end of monarchy. The turmoil that followed ended in King Tribhuvan fleeing from house arrest to India in 1950. The King signed the 1950 Indo-Nepal Treaty of Peace and Friendship that established a close Indo-Nepalese relationship on commerce, defence and foreign relations. India in return helped to restore the monarchy. The Treaty was resented by some political parties of Nepal. Many in Nepal saw it as an encroachment of its sovereignty and an unwelcome extension of Indian influence. The deployment of an Indian military mission in Nepal in the 1950s increased these concerns.

In 1959, Tribhuvan's son King Mahendra issued a new constitution in an attempt to control the pro-democracy movement. The first elections for a national assembly were held in 1960. The Nepali Congress Party gained a substantial victory in the election. Its leader, B P Koirala formed a government and served as prime minister. However, the democratic government was short lived. In 1962, King Mahendra declared parliamentary democracy as a failure. He dismissed the elected Koirala government and declared that a party less "panchayet" system would govern Nepal. He promulgated a new constitution. The elected Prime Minister, Members of Parliament and hundreds of activists supporting democracy were arrested. This trend of arrest of political activists and democracy supporters continued for 30 years.

In 1979, King Birendra called for a national referendum to decide on the nature of Nepal's government. The referendum was held in May 1980. The "panchayat" system won a narrow victory. The king carried out the promised reforms including selection of the prime minister by the Rastriya Panchayat. There was relative peace till a dispute with India led to India's closing of most border crossings between India and Nepal from March 1989 to July 1990. **In 1990, the Nepali Congress along with leftist parties decided to launch a decisive movement for multi-party parliamentary democracy. The movement forced the monarchy to accept constitutional reforms and to establish a multi-party parliament. In May 1991, Nepal**

held its first parliamentary elections in nearly 30 years. The Nepali Congress won 110 of the 205 seats and formed the first elected government in 32 years. Mid-term elections in November 1994, which were called after the government lost a parliamentary vote, resulted in a hung parliament and the communists, who emerged as the single largest party, formed a minority government.

A Maoist insurgency broke out in Nepal in 1996. The civil war between Maoists and the Nepalese government began in 1996. The army was called in 2001. Peace talks in 2001 and 2003 were unsuccessful. By 2005 the Maoists had control over an estimated 40 to 60 percent of the country. Most of the rural population supported the insurgents. King Birendra was assassinated in 2004. His brother Gyanendra became king. King Gyanendra dissolved the Parliament in 2005 and assumed direct rule to suppress the Maoist insurgency. **In 2006, anti-monarchy cum pro-democracy forces and Maoists came together. Maoists came over ground. King Gyanendra was forced to abdicate and the Monarchy was dissolved in 2008.**

National elections were held in Nepal in 2008. A Maoist led government came to power through a coalition. The Maoists had announced their intentions to renegotiate Nepal's 1950 treaty with India. Nepal has a difficult task balancing its relations with China and India.

Nepal's Relations with China

Nepal invaded Tibet, which was a part of China, for the second time in 1854. China intervened and defeated the Nepalese. The Treaty of Thapathali was signed between the two in March 1856. The treaty recognized the China's suzerainty over Tibet and Nepal agreed to pay annual feudatory tribute. Relations between Nepal and China and Tibet continued without any major incident until 1904, when British India sent an armed expedition to Tibet. Nepal rejected Tibet's request for aid. Nepal stopped paying tribute to China in 2008. China reasserted its claim over Tibet in 1910. Nepal broke relations with China when the Tibetans, taking advantage of the Chinese revolution of 1911, drove the Chinese out.

China occupied Tibet in 1950. It also increased its support for the Communist Party of Nepal. This led to break in diplomatic relations between Kathmandu and Beijing. Diplomatic relations were restored in 1955. The two nations signed a new treaty in 1956 terminating the Treaty of Thapathali of 1856. Nepal recognized Tibet as a part of China but payment of tribute stopped. **In 1961, Nepal and China signed a boundary settlement agreement and a treaty of peace and friendship. China has**

built an all-weather road connecting the Nepalese capital Kathmandu with Tibet starting 1961. The highway is of great strategic value to China. Nepal remained neutral during the Sino-Indian War of 1962. In the 1970s King Birendra proposed Nepal as a "zone of peace" between India and China.

The Khampas had been waging an armed freedom struggle with funds and assistance from CIA. They had secretly created their base in Mustang (north-west Nepal). In early 1970s, the US President started wooing China and stopped CIA aid to the Khampas. In 1974, the Nepalese Army, under Chinese pressure, mobilized and disarmed the Tibetan Khampas.

Chinese leader Deng Xiaoping visited Kathmandu in 1977. **Sino-Nepalese relations received a major boost in 2004 when King Gyanendra took over power. The US, UK and India had refused to supply arms to the regime alleging human rights violations. China stepped in and supplied arms to Nepal. The military relations and economic cooperation between China and Nepal have been improving ever since. Visits were exchanged between Army Chiefs and Defence Secretaries of Nepal and China.**

Economic Relations

The bilateral economic and trade relations between Nepal and have been improving since 1977. The two Governments agreed to set up an Economic and Trade Joint Committee in 1983. In 2001, the two countries signed the Memorandum of Understanding on Tourism Cooperation. They also signed an "Air Service Agreement", according to which, Air China and Nepal airlines opened a direct air link between China and Nepal in 2004. Nepal's total volume of trade with China increased from US$157 million in 2003 to US$ 268 million in 2006. The Chinese Government has been granting concessional loans to Nepal. The total number of Chinese investment projects in Nepal had reached 30 by 2007. In 2007-08, China has constructed a 770 km railway line connecting Lhasa with the Nepalese border town of Khasa. Until now, the Chinese Government has assisted Nepal to undertake many projects including about 400 km of highways, Seti River bridge at Pokara, seven industrial projects, Sunkoshi Hydroelectric Project, Pokhara Water Conservancy and Irrigation Project and a number of education and healthcare projects.

Strategic Relations

China has been trying to reduce Indian influence on the Nepalese Army. Nepalese Army has sent officers and soldiers to study in Chinese military universities since 1998. China has been sending its military officers to participate in the adventure trainings organized by the Nepal Army since 2002. China will provide 62.5 million rupees as military aid to Nepal in 2008. China has provided Nepal with a large number of armoured personnel carriers air defence guns.

China has Nepal in a debt trap with its Belt Road projects in Nepal. Chinese shops are common in Kathmandu as are hoardings and signposts in Chinese language. However, its influence has weaned a bit with the Communists losing power. Chinese encroachment of a small but strategic strip of border area with Tibet. This is resented by the locals. But the Nepalese Government is too weak to do anything but protest.

Nepalese Armed Forces

The Nepalese Army was reorganized into divisions in 2001. There was considerable expansion in the period 2004-06 to fight the Maoist rebels. Nepal has six combat divisions. It is estimated that in 2003 the army had about 85,000 active-duty personnel, including nearly 320 personnel in the Royal Nepal Army Air Wing. **The Indian army has 40,000 Nepalese in its Gurkha regiments.** As of January 2005, Nepal was the world's fourth largest contributor of troops to UN peacekeeping missions with 3,016 troops serving in various international peacekeeping operations.

The army is believed to have a mix of weapon systems from India, China, UK, Pakistan and Russia. Nepal and China signed a $2.6 million military aid pact. There has been many such deals since.

Nepal's has been trying to maintain equal distance with China and India while simultaneously trying to reduce India's influence and Nepal's dependence on India. Further, Kathmandu seems to believe that the competition between its two giant neighbours, China and India, would benefit its own economic development.

Chinese and Pakistani influence in Nepal has been increasing. India has been unable to match Chinese aid to Nepal. It also has problems on its border with Nepal in Terrai region and near Dharchula in Uttarakhand. One does not know whether such a move will be resisted by the Nepalese Army. Like all of India's neighbours, Nepal is more of a problem than an asset.

Summary

Nepal never had good relations with India except during the period 1950 to 2005. Nepalese resented India's big brother attitude and interference in Nepalese politics. The Chinese made their entry into Nepal in 1961. Lately it has taken advantage of Communist Party rule in Nepal and increased its influence. It has also used its money power to

help Nepal develop economically.

China has extended its road network into Tibet. It also has extended its railway system upto Nepal's border with Tibet. These can be used by the PLA to attack India.

Analysis

Nepal has neither the capability nor will to prevent its territory being used by China to wage war on India. They only way we can permanently secure our northern border is to help Tibetans liberate Tibet.

CHAPTER NINE

China's Build-up in Tibet

Tibet Autonomous Region (TAR) and the Xinjiang Province of China are sensitive regions. Tibetans and the Uighur Muslims of Xinjiang have secessionist ambitions and have a history of violent protests. Tibetan refugees and Dalai Lama's presence in India, presence of Taliban and Al Qaeda on China's western borders only makes the situation worse. **China therefore maintains a large military force in the region. It has developed the capability to quickly induct troops by road, railway and air from military bases anywhere in China. Lhasa is virtually surrounded by military camps and the inner city has a heavy presence of special armed police and under-cover security personnel.**

Chinese military presence in Tibet has grave strategic implications for India.

Infrastructure Development in Tibet

China has been improving the connectivity between main land China and Tibet ever since it annexed Tibet in 1950. By the end of 2003, some 41,302 km of roads had been completed. To date, the region has five national-level, 14 regional level and six lateral or inter connecting highways, which basically satisfy the social and economic development needs of Tibet. In addition to the 3,200 km of asphalted roads, 32,195 km of rural roads have also been built, linking some 683 townships and 5,956 villages across the region. These have been a boon for travellers and bus companies who today serve 627 townships and 4,214 villages. It has also built five networks of roads leading to its borders with India and Nepal. These are described below.

The Western Highway or the Xinjiang -Tibet Highway. This network starts at Amdo and passes through Silling - Aksai Chin and connects Tibet with Xinjiang Province's road-network at Mazar. This road is being used to sustain the 50,000 plus troops that China has amassed to enforce its territorial claims in Ladakh.

Qinghai-Tibet Highway. This network is Tibet's longest asphalt paved road. It stretches from Xinning, the capital city of Qinghai Province to Lhasa. It has gradual gradients and is of high quality. It is the safest road to Tibet.

Sichuan-Tibet Highway. This highway runs between Chengdu, the capital city of Sichuan Province and Lhasa. Sichuan-Tibet Highway is probably the most dangerous highway in the world. It has two branches. The North Route is about 2,400 km long and the South Route of about 2,100 km. It runs across a variety of rivers and mountains with the highest point over 5,000 m above sea level. Landslides are frequent. The road is very susceptible to attack by the Indian Air Force or disruption by Tibetan resistance.

The Yunnan-Tibet Highway. This highway connects Yunnan Province to Tibet. It skirts Arunachal Pradesh from the East and will be used if China decides to attack Lohit or Subansari districts of Arunachal Pradesh or for moving troops from Yunnan Province to Tibet.

The Sino-Nepal Highway is the only international highway in Tibet. It connects Lhasa to Kathmandu. Most of the highways in the Tibet region will be within striking range of the Su-30MKI fighters when deployed by India. If China were to have a military confrontation with India, highway transport could be more reliable than the Qinghai-Tibet railway which could be more easily damaged and difficult to repair.

Highway S 207. This highway runs east from Shigatse up to Jiangrexiang and then turns south towards Chumbi valley and Dokalam. This is the main supply route for troops deployed opposite Sikkim and Western Bhutan.

Highway G 318/G 4218. This starts at Yaan in Sichuan Province of China and runs west along the border with Arunachal Pradesh and on to Lasha.

Highway G 219. This highway starts at Lasha and runs west via Shigatse all along the border with India. It turns north on crossing the Indus River and enters Aksai Chin and goes to Xinjian. This is the main supply route for Chinese troops deployed opposite Uttarakhand, Himachal Pradesh and Ladakh.

Other Infrastructure

The Qinghai-Tibet railway is the longest and highest plateau-based railroad in the world. It has a total length of 1,956 km and connects Xining in Qinghai Province and Lhasa in the Tibet Autonomous Region. It was completed in 2006. The "Tibet Railway" refers to the section from Golmud to Lhasa and runs for 1,142 km and passes through mostly uninhabited zones. The Tibet Railway itself with 675 bridges is marvel to behold. The main stations on the line are Xining, Delinga, Golmud, Amdo, Nakchu, Damxung, Lhasa. There are plans to extend the railway line from Lhasa to Katmandu. This will indeed have geopolitical ramifications for India. China claims that the annual transport capacity of the railway was 5 million tons per year or about 14,000 tons per day.

The Golmud - Lhasa pipeline has a capacity of half a million tons of fuel annually. With the completion of the Qinghai-Tibet railway line, China will be able to overcome a major obstacle to increasing its military deployment near the India-Tibet border region. Some consider that the rail link gives China the capability to induct up to 12 divisions a month into Tibet.

Tibet has 25 airfields and air strips. All the airfields in Tibet have been lengthened and upgraded. Many air bases have been built. Currently only four are in active use but others can be activated in a short period of time. **China's PLAAF has fourteen military airfields and bases in Tibet. These are Taxcorgan, Ngari-Gunsa, Burang, Tingri, Shigatse, Lasha-Gongar, Damxung, Lhuntse, Hoping, Pangta, Shiquanhe, and Kong Ka. Of these Ngari-Gunsa, Shigatse and Lhuntse are withing 60 km of Tibet's border with China.**

Military build-up on the Tibetan plateau

The whole of Tibet has been put under two military regions, the Chengdu Military Region with its headquarters at Chengdu and the Lanzhou Military Region with its headquarters at Lanzhou. (See Google Maps).

Chengdu Military region is responsible for Tibet Autonomous Region or TAR and Sichuan and Yunnan Provinces. Lanzhou Military Region is responsible for operations in Xinjiang Province, Aksai Chin and Qinghai Province. The strength of Chinese military personnel in Tibet is estimated to be around 500,000.

The Chegdu Military Region consists of three Group Armies (the 13th, 14th and 54th), the Tibetan 52nd and 53d Mountain Brigades, the 149th Motorised Infantry Division at Leshan, Sichuan, two Mobile Armed Police Divisions (38th and 41st), and the 2nd Army Aviation Regiment at Chengdu. The No. 52 Brigade, stationed at Linzhi, is highly mechanized and armed with T-92 wheeled armoured vehicles and HJ-8/9 anti-tank missiles. The No. 53 Mountain Brigade is stationed at Milin and is also the PLA combat unit stationed closest to the city of Lhasa. **However, deployments keep changing with change of command and operational plans. The figures are only to give the readers and idea and not for planning operations.**

There are six sub-military districts in the TAR. TAR is estimated to have two independent infantry brigades (Tibetan 52 and 53 Mountain Brigades), six border defence regiments, five independent border defence battalions, three artillery regiments, three engineers' regiments, one main signal station and two signal regiments, three transport regiments and three independent transport battalions, four air force bases, two radar regiments, and a regiment of para-military forces. It also has two division (38th and 41st) and six independent regiments of People's Armed Police. In addition, there are 12 units of what is known as the "second artillery (or the strategic nuclear missile) division". The People's Armed Police are regular PLA troops re-designated as such recently. The front line troop concentrations in the TAR are said to be located at Ruthok, Gyamuk, Drongpa, Saga, Drangso (Dhingri), Gampa-la, Dromo, Tsona, Lhuntse Dzong, Zayul, etc close to the LAC. The second line of defences are concentrated at Shigatse, Lhasa, Nagchukha, Tsethang, Nangartse, Gyamdha, Nyingtri, Powo Tramo, Tsawa Pomdha, Chamdo, etc. In addition, China regularly deploys the Sichuan based 149 Motorized Division in the TAR, as it did in the wake of the Tibetan demonstrations in Lhasa in 1987 and thereafter. **China is also planning to shift the headquarters of the TAR Military District from Chengdu to a site located to the southwest of Lhasa, along the road to Gongkar airport.** The move may have been completed.

Xinjiang and Qinghai come under Lanzhou Military Region. It has the 61st Rapid Reaction Division stationed at Tianshui and the 12 Armored Division, stationed at Zhangye in Gansu province. The 4th Motorized Infantry Division of Xinjiang Military Region is located quite close to the Afghanistan border. The 6th Motorized Infantry Division, stationed at Kashi, is the only mechanized combat unit in the Xinjiang Military Region. It is also close to Afghanistan and is located right in the heart of southern Xinjiang. Should Uighur independence activities break out of control, the above two divisions would be the first to be dispatched. Urumqi, the capital of Xinjiang, it is under the 11th Brigade. 26th Group Army is stationed in the Xinjiang Military Sub Region. The 63 Armed Police Division and 7 Infantry Division are under the 21st Group Army and are stationed at the cities of Pingliang and Ili, respectively. The largest military bases in Tibet under Lanzhou Military Region are at Silling, Chabcha, and Karmu. All the three places also have air force bases. Golmud is also a major military base. Located strategically to cover both Tibet and Eastern Turkestan, this region is connected by road, rail and air.

The Chinese military build-up in Kham and Ngapa regions are concentrated in Lithang, Kanze, Tawu, Dartsedo, etc, in Kham sub-district, and Barkham in Ngapa sub-district. However, there are radar stations and dormant air strips in Kham sub-district at various localities.

China has deployed over 50,000 troops in occupied Aksai Chin. Sources say the listening stations will monitor Indian deployments in the region, eavesdrop on forward and intelligence communications of the army. **It must be noted that the deployments are mainly around major population areas like Lasha and Shigatse and other towns and to protect borders where threat is perceived. Deployment also caters for protection of strategically important highways.**

Mobilization

China could move one rapid reaction division from the Chengdu Military Region and one rapid reaction division, the 61st Plateau Rapid Reaction Motorized Division of No. 26 Group Army under the Lanzhou Military Region to Tibet to meet any emergency within days. Some additional airborne troops, rapid reaction troops and armed police could be directly delivered to Lhasa from the air. The No. 15 Airborne Division could be air-dropped to Tibet and equipment such as airborne fighting vehicles could be put to use. China will need to induct another six to eight divisions for launching any major offensive. That could take at least a month. **With China's present preoccupation with Taiwan and South China sea, it may be difficult for China to send additional military resources to Tibet.**

Nuclear Weapons

China has nuclear installations and testing facilities in Northern Tibet. The first nuclear weapon was brought onto the Tibetan plateau in 1971 and stationed in the Tsai dam basin, in the north eastern district of Amdo. As China's ground-based nuclear missiles can be transported and fired from trailers, efforts to locate and count missiles in certain areas remain difficult.

China's primary weapon research and design facility, known as the "Ninth Academy" is located in Haiyan in Amdo District. It was responsible for designing all of China's nuclear bombs through the mid-seventies. It also served as a research centre for detonation development, radiochemistry and many other nuclear weapons related activities. China is believed to have nuclear manufacturing centres at Haiyan and Huangyuan in Amdo.

China will be very sensitive to any sabotage or attack on any of these installations.

Missiles

The Chinese have deployed a large number of missiles in Tibet. Most of these are targeted at Indian cities. It is reported that there are eight missile bases containing at least eight ICBMs, seventy MRBMs, twenty IRBMs and 17 Radar Stations in TAR. The missile bases are located to the south of Lake Kokonor in Amdo and Nagchukha. China has established a nuclear missile deployment and launch site for DF-4 missiles (China's first inter-continental ballistic missile) in the Tsai Dam basin at Haiyan. Another nuclear missile site in Tibet is located at Delingha, about 200 km southeast of Larger Tsai Dam. It also houses DF-4s and is the missile regimental headquarters for Amdo. A new nuclear division has also been established in Amdo. Four CSS-4 missiles are reported to be based there, which have a range of 8000 miles, capable of striking the United States, Europe and all of Asia.

Summary

China has developed the communications and road networks in Tibet. This network would be very useful for moving its armed forces in times of war. The roads, railways, pipelines and telecommunication infrastructures are very long and pass through sparsely populated and most inhospitable terrain.

China has deployed a very large force in Tibet to cater for internal violent protests and for operations against India.

Analysis

Tibet is a vast mountainous country which is sparsely populated. Areas around Lasha and Sighatse and those in Amdo region bordering China ware relatively more developed. The Kham region which borders Arunachal and Sikkim and Western Tibet which borders Ladakh, Himachal and Uttarakhand States of India are relatively less populated. **The terrain, particularly in the regions of Nanda Devi, Kanchenjunga and Arunachal is very mountainous and difficult. They are ideal for establishing bases for the Tibetan Liberation Army.**

In spite of the improved infrastructure, the Chinese Army will have serious operational problems in Tibet. These are listed below.

- **Long axes of maintenance** which can be disrupted by weather, Tibetan resistance and enemy action.

- **Requirement of acclimatization of troops** and adverse effects of high altitude on men, animals and material.
- **A sullen local population** not reconciled to Chinese occupation.
- **Reduced airlift capability** due to high altitude conditions.

Grant of asylum to Dalai Lama and his followers after his flight to India in 1959 is seen as a hostile act by China. China feels that the Khampa rebellion of 1959 was aided and abetted by India in collusion with Western powers. Establishment of Tibetan government in exile in India has only aggravated matters. **Efforts by the Dalai Lama to keep alive the issue of Tibetan independence/autonomy and seek world support further angered the Chinese.** China follows a policy of zero tolerance to disruptive activities in TAR and Xinjiang. It therefore maintains adequate troops in the region.

Tibet, irrespective of China's tight control remains volatile. Although the Dalai Lama has relinquished his demand for total independence, his continued stay in India and the large support he enjoys in the Western World will keep the pot boiling. How this issue is finally resolved will have a major bearing on Sino-India relations.

The Tibetan youth are getting restless and are convinced that the non-violent movement is being seen as Tibetan weakness and would not lead to any tangible results. Tibetan youth may well adopt the Indian model of seeking independence from British rule through the combination of non-violent and violent movements. So long as China perceives that India is supporting the Tibetan movement, it will always be suspicious of Indian motives and an uneasy peace will continue to prevail between these neighbours. **If unrest spreads in Tibet, China may adopt the option of going to war with India and try to settle the problem once for all. However, China is currently heavily involved with unification of Taiwan and asserting its claim on South China sea. Under the circumstances it is unlikely that it can spare military resources for an all-out war with India.**

It will also be seen that the main Group Armies of Chengdu Military Region which is responsible for operations in TAR, the 54th, 13th and 14th are not located in TAR but in Sichuan and Yunnan Provinces in peace time. This is primarily for administrative and logistic convenience. Troops within TAR are mainly of holding and defensive nature. Any major offensive through Tibet will require induction of additional troops from Lanzhou and other Military Regions possibly Beijing or Jinan Military Regions which are connected by rail to Tibet. However, there are many logistic bases in

Tibet which holds requirements of ammunitions, rations, fuel, equipment and spares that may be required for a war. **The best way to tie down Chinese Forces in Tibet is to get them involved in a guerrilla war. A few hundred Pakistan trained terrorist have tied down over 100,000 security personnel in J&K. Imagine the problems a few thousand well-armed and trained Tibetan freedom fighters could pose to the Chinese army in the far more hostile and under-developed regions of Tibet.**

CHAPTER TEN

Understanding Chinese Armed Forces

China's Defence Budget

China's defence budget for 2022 was about US$ 230 billion. This is only next to the US and vastly larger than any other country than Russia. In real terms, the budget could be more than that of the US for the following reasons:

- **The cost of production in China is much less than in the US or EU.** China produces most of its military equipment including aircraft carriers, war ships, submarines, aircraft, missile systems, tanks, armoured vehicles, radars and other communication systems. They have access to most of Russian technology.
- **Salaries and perks of Chinese soldiers would be about one seventh of the US soldiers.**

China's Weapon Systems

China produces almost every weapon system that is needed during war. The short comings in terms of quality it makes up with quantity.

The Chinese Soldier

This is the main weakness of the Chinese Armed Forces. Because of the one child policy, **every Chinese in the armed forces is an only child. Death of the only son is a family disaster. Hence, the will to fight in hostile foreign soil is low.**

The other problem is that most Chinese soldiers are conscript soldiers. All males in China in the age bracket of 18-22 have to register for military service. Not all are taken. Conscripts are selected from volunteers. **Conscripts serve for three years in the Army and 4 years in the navy** and air force. This short tenure is not enough for collective training at section, platoon, company and battalion level. Building regimental spirit or bonding which is the primary motivation for infantry, armoured corps and engineers who have to fight enemy troops at close quarters is completely missing. Fear of punishment is the only motivation for fighting.

Chinese soldiers have never been fired at by artillery, air craft or even small arms sine 1979 when they fought the Vietnamese. No one knows how they will react when they come under fire and have to pick up the dead and the wounded.

China's War Record

China has never fought a war since 1979 when they attempted a punitive expedition in Vietnam where they were soundly defeated. **Chinese commanders have no war experience.**

Analysis

China is arguably the world's number one economic power. It may not have the largest investment capital, the highest GDP or per capita income in the world. **But it has the world highest foreign exchange reserve of about $ 3.2 trillion which is more than twice that of Japan, four times that of EU, five times that of Russia and about six times that of India.** This huge foreign exchange reserves enables China to access technology and natural resources all over the world and buy political influence in our neighbouring countries through economic and military aid. **China is also the largest holder of US treasury bonds and US debt. It can destabilize the dollar whenever it chooses to by simply redeeming the US Treasury Bonds or selling a few billion US dollars on the world's foreign exchange markets.** China has been demanding that the US dollar should be replaced by an SDR as the worlds trading currency. China has prevented the Asian Development Bank from providing a loan to India for development of Arunachal Pradesh.

China wants to dethrone the US as the worlds no 1 power, If it is left to progress unhindered, there is no doubt that they will become the world's number one military power. Time to stop China is now.

China under President Xi Jinping is now at its belligerent best. After seventy-one years of deception, China has finally made its position clear.China will not rest till it has taken all territory of its neighbours that it claimed by drawing lines and hashes on world map in 1959. It will use threats of use of force or use economic leverage to get what it wants. The gullible presidents of the United States of America from Richards Nixon

1970 to Barack Obama 2016, at the behest of their greedy multinational corporations, shifted manufacturing and investment to China and made it rich and militarily powerful. **Now, after the Centenary celebrations of the Chinese Communist Party in 2021, its President Xi Jinping is pushing hard to capture all territories claimed by China in 1959.** Pakistan, Kazakhstan and Nepal have already ceded the territory demanded. Bhutan and Taiwan have been put on notice. Hong Kong is no longer autonomous. Military facilities have been created on disputed islands in the South China Sea. Vietnam, Malaysia, Philippines and Indonesia have been asked to cede their claims in the South China Sea. Japanese territorial waters are being violated by Chinese coast guard vessels. A flotilla of thousands of Chinese fishing vessels is prowling the Pacific Ocean close to the coast of South America. The Chinese Army has deployed in strength on its border with India, threatening to enforce its claims by force. It has also declared that it does not recognize Ladakh to be a part of India. Naval and combined arms drills are being regularly held to try to cow down Taiwan and other South China Sea rim nations.

Time to take on China is now. The timid and the cowardly political leaders will always delay taking a strong stand against aggressive behaviour by neighbours hoping that better sense will prevail. Any delay widens the gap in military capability between China and India and most of its neighbours. China's defence budget is second only to the US. Hence the gap between its military strength and that of its neighbours increases every year. Thus, delay in resisting China will only make it more difficult to do so.

CHAPTER ELEVEN

Helping Tibetans Liberate Tibet

Tibetan Armed Resistance 1958 to 1973

Resistance to the Chinese occupation of Tibet started in 1950. Khampas and Amdowas fought against the occupying Chinese PLA since 1956 in different parts of Kham and Amdo regions of Tibet. The remnants of the Tibetan army and Khampas took to the remote areas and kept engaging the Chinese Army in hit and raids. They operated in small isolated groups with no central command or coordination. **General Andrug Gompo Tashi brought them together and established the Chushi Gangdrup freedom fighters.** He financed many of the fighters and was accepted as the undisputed leader of the resistance army. Later, the force was joined by members of the Tibetan Army and volunteers. The force was equipped with World War II vintage British 303, German and Russian 7.62 mm rifles and some grenades. **They escorted the Dalai Lama in his flight to India in 1959 and then handed over their weapons and ammunitions to the Indian Administration.**

The struggle was revived with CIA help in 1959. A Tibetan guerrilla base was established in Mustang, Nepal in 1960 with CIA aid. About 2,000 fighters, mostly ethnic Khampas gathered there. By spring 1961, Mustang guerrilla units had begun raids on isolated Chinese posts. CIA trained five small groups and parachuted them into different areas of Tibet. These groups did not prove very effective. **Years passed without the Tibetan Resistance being able to intensify operations or establish any bases inside Tibet.** US support for the Mustang fighters dwindled. Arms drops ceased in 1965. Without support from India and the US, the poorly armed Tibetan resistance struggled to survive. The CIA provided the government-in-exile money to open offices in Geneva and New York. They also helped resettlement of Tibetan orphans in Switzerland. President Nixon stopped the assistance to the freedom fighters in 1973. The fighters laid down their arms on directions of the Dalai Lama. **The movement finally ended in 1973 when US President** <u>Richard Nixon</u> **decided to seek rapprochement with** <u>China</u>.

Tibetans in Exile

There are about 150,000 Tibetans living outside Tibet. That amounts to about 2% of the population of about 6 million. Most of them are in India. **The Central Tibetan Administration (CTA),** based at Dharmshala, India looks after their needs and administers Tibetan institutions in India and abroad. About 4000 Tibetans work for the administration and a number of schools, institutions, settlements and business. The Dokham Chushi Gangdruk organization, is now a charity set up in New York and India with chapters in other countries. They now provide financial support to survivors of the Chushi Gangdruk Resistance Army led by Andrug Gompo Tashi currently living in India.

The Middle Way Approach

The Dalai Lama's brother, Gyalo Thondup was advised by Chinese President Deng Xiaoping in 1979 that all issues except total independence can be resolved through negotiations. This encouraged the Dalai Lama to pursue negotiations for a mutually beneficial and peaceful solution instead of fighting to restore independence. He sent three fact finding missions into Tibet and wrote a personal letter to the Chinese President Deng Xiaoping. He sent representatives to Beijing in 1982 to start negotiations. Their Chinese counterparts were not interested in discussing the situation in Tibet. The Dalai Lama sent 6 delegations to China. **In 1987, the Dalai Lama unveiled the Five Point Peace Plan as a "first step towards a lasting solution". The five points were:**

- **The whole of Tibet should be transformed into a zone of peace.**
- **China's population transfer policy which threatened the very existence of the Tibetans as a people must stop.**
- **The fundamental human rights and democratic freedoms of the Tibetan people must be respected.**
- **Restoration and protection of Tibet's natural environment should be ensured and China should stop use of Tibet for the production of nuclear weapons and dumping of nuclear waste.**

- **China must start negotiations on the future status of Tibet and of relations between the Tibetan and Chinese peoples.**

Periodic meetings between the CTA's envoys and the Chinese government took place without any progress. The CTA suspended meetings 1994. They resumed at the pace of one per year between 2002 and 2008. **Again, there was no progress as China stuck to its "My way or no way" policy.**

The CTA claims that the Middle Way Approach enjoys widespread support from the international community. The Middle Way approach has been supported and lauded by the US and the West. **China has stubbornly refused to accept the Middle Way Approach. Things got worse for the Tibetan People after Xi Jinping became China's President in 2013.**

Pro-independence Protests 1987 to date

Many pro-independence protests took place in Tibet after September 1987. Some are listed below:

- **On March 5, 1989, a group of monks, nuns and ordinary people took to the streets in Lasha to celebrate the 30th anniversary of the 1959 Tibetan Uprising and the escape of Dalai Lama.** Police and Chinese security personnel tried to put down the protests, Tensions escalated and even greater crowd of protesters took to the streets. Protests turned violent. More than 1200 Chinese shops, offices, and residences were burned, and fire was set to nearly 100 cars, including police vehicles. Martial law was declared on March 8, 1989 after 3 days of protests. Foreign journalists and tourists were expelled. Over a 100 Tibetans were killed and thousands were arrested. The number of the Chinese security personnel and Han Chinese settlers killed was not disclosed. Violent protests also took place in Gansu Province. Tibetans burnt down homes and shops of Han and Hui settlers before the security forces arrived.

- **Large-scale and coordinated protests erupted during the Olympic Torch Relay for Beijing Olympics in 2008. In India, a group of Tibetan exile organizations like Tibetan Youth Congress, Tibetan Women's Association, Students for a Free Tibet and National Democratic Party of Tibet etc. started a "Return March to Tibet" carrying Tibetan Flags.** They planned to reach Tibet on foot just in time for the opening of the Olympic Games. The CTA tried to dissuade the marchers but failed. The group was stopped and arrested by the Indian police.

- **Over 150 monks have self-immolated for Tibetan Independence since 2009.** A wave of self-immolations by Tibetans in China, India and Nepal occurred after the Phuntsog self-immolation incident of 2011. The Dalai Lama has said he does not encourage the protests. But he has praised the courage of those who engage in self-immolation. He blamed the cases of self-immolations on "cultural genocide" by the Chinese. The Chinese Premier said that such extreme actions hurt social harmony. At the same time he reiterated that Tibet and the Tibetan areas of Sichuan are integral parts of Chinese territory.

To Fight for Freedom or Not

The present Dalai Lama officially announced retirement from his role as the political leader of the CTA in March 2011. The Prime Minister elect thus became the highest-ranking political office of the CTA. Dalai Lama is now a purely religious leader. Dr. Lobsang Sangay, a graduate of Harvard Law School who was born in a refugee camp in India in 1968 was named Prime Minister of the CTA on April 27, 2011. He thus succeeded the Dalai Lama as the political leader of the Tibetan cause. **Sangay, was once a militant leader of the Tibetan Youth Congress which unequivocally supports Tibetan independence. However, Sangay claimed that he has matured and now supports the Middle Way Approach.** Dr. Sangay served for two terms as Prime Minister of the CTA and retired in May 2021. **Penpa Tshering won the election and has taken over charge as head of CTA from Dr. Sangay in May 2921. He served as the North America Representative of Dalai Lama for a year in 2016 and would be no stranger to the US Administration and CIA. He also supports the Middle Way Path to achieve autonomy for Tibet. That may not be a very encouraging sign for the six million colonized and brutalized Tibetans living in Tibet. The Tibetans in Tibet will have to find a way to organize armed resistance to Chinese occupation.**

Tibet can be Liberated only if Tibetans are Ready to Fight for Independence

The world or even India cannot be realistically expected to launch a military operation like the Korean War or even India's military operations to liberate East Pakistan and creation of Bangladesh. China is a major nuclear power and the resources required for launching military operations against it are just too much. The free world can at best help Tibetans fight a liberation struggle. The US and NATO assisted the liberation of Croatia, Bosnia Herzegovina and Kosovo. They also helped Libyans to remove the dictatorship of Gaddafi. The US and its allies have been assisting Syrian rebels fight the regime of President Assad. Some nations of Europe have been assisting the Kurds in their struggle against Turkey. Pakistan has been supporting armed struggle in Indian Kashmir. China has been supporting the armed insurgencies in India's North Eastern States. So, **assisting the Tibetans to fight for independence would be a normal geopolitical game for the US and its allies and even India with plenty of precedence.**

The Tibetan government in exile, the Central Tibetan Administration (CTA), under the influence of the present Dalai Lama, has changed the goal of its struggle from full independence to the "Middle Way Approach or cooperation with China with political and religious autonomy". It seeks "genuine autonomy for all Tibetans living in the three traditional provinces of Tibet within the framework of the People's Republic of China". However, negotiations on the issue have not produced any result. **It is foolish for the CTA to think that China will concede that demand. China's objective is clear. The demography of Tibet will be changed. Its culture and Buddhism will be obliterated.**

Not all exiled Tibetans are content with pursuing the current CTA policy of the Middle Way Approach and many expressed their frustration in 2008, against the Dalai Lama's wishes, by agitating for independence. The present Dalai Lama announced his retirement from political life in 2011. Hence it is for the new Prime Minister of the Central Tibetan Authority to decide whether to pursue full independence or not. **The Prime Minister and his cabinet must decide whether the struggle for autonomy or full independence should remain non-violent or be a combination of civil disobedience and non-cooperation and armed struggle.** That was the model India followed. On one side Mahatma Gandhi and the Congress party launched non-violent agitation asking the British to quit. On the other side, Netaji Subhash Chandra Bose and his Indian National Army, freedom fighters like Bhagat Sing took up arms against the British. **Whatever be the decision, there is no need for the CTA to make the decision public.**

The CTA and the world must remember that Tibet could enjoy independence whenever mainland China was faced with internal problems. The first period was from 1562 to 1644 when the Han Chinese Ming Dynasty and the Manchus fought for supremacy. The second was from 1911 to 1950 when the Qing Dynasty was weakened by a number of rebellions and finally collapsed leading to the formation of the People's Republic of China. **China is currently beset with multiple problems.** Its relations with the US and Japan are at their lowest over Taiwan; crack-down on pro-democracy movement in Hong Kong and over territorial claims in South China Sea; human rights abuses and cultural genocide of Uighurs in Xinjiang. Its economy is crippled by COVID related lockdowns, unprecedented drought in the Yangtse River basin, severe floods in southern China, collapse of real-estate market and liquidity problem in some of its banks. **Now is the time to try to liberate Tibet.**

Instances of Armed Freedom Struggles

There are many instances when countries have successfully fought freedom struggles against their colonizers. **Nationalist leader of Indonesia declared independence in August 1945.** The Dutch tried to re-establish their rule. Four years of armed freedom struggle ended in December 1949, when the Dutch formally recognised Indonesian independence. **The armed freedom struggle started in Malaysia in 1948 and ended on 31 August 1957. The armed struggle for independence in Vietnam lasted from 1946 to 1954 when the Viet Minh defeated the French colonizers in the Battle of Dien Bien Phou or for 8 years. The armed struggle for freedom in Kenya lasted from 1952 to 1962.** It will be seen that armed freedom struggles do not usually win quick victories. Many lives have to be sacrificed before the colonial power gets exhausted and concedes independence. Armed struggle for political and religious autonomy may be easier to achieve.

Conditions Required for Successful Armed Struggles

The outcome of armed struggles depends on certain factors. These are listed below:

- **Appeal for the Cause.** The cause could be total independence or political andreligious autonomy. It must have the support of the majority of people of Tibet or of the region to be liberated like southern Tibet, Kham Region or Amdo region. **The fact that the Chushi Gangdruk armed Tibetan resistance was active from 1958 to 1973 and protests against Chinese occupation continue to flare up even today clearly indicate that the people of Tibet want independence or at least political and religious autonomy.**
- **Popular Support.** The cause must have active support of the region. Just as the fish cannot live outside water, the freedom fighters must have the

support of the local population. It is the local population that provides freedom fighters, rations and food and most importantly, information about the enemy locations, strengths and movements. **The cases of self-immolation and periodic protests against the Chinese indicates that there is support for a freedom movement in Tibet. Active support of 10 percent of the population is usually adequate for a successful struggle.** It is the people who bear the brunt of the atrocities of the armed forces of the occupiers.

- **Quality of Leadership.** Freedom fighters need good leadership. The leader must be charismatic and be able to lead by example. They must have a good knowledge of military tactics and strategy and human skills. **Mao De dzong, Netaji Subhash Bose, President Suharto, Ho Chi Minh were some of the memorable leaders.** The CTA will have to identify a few leaders like General Andrug Gompo Tashi who started the Chushi Gangdrup freedom movement and provide them necessary support. **The Special Frontier Force described later could be a source of top and middle level military leaders.**

- **Military Efficiency.** The success of the freedom struggle will also depend on the military efficiency of the freedom fighters. **Military efficiency comes from morale, training in use of arms, communication systems, medical aid, tactics; arms including hand held anti-tank and anti-aircraft weapons; support equipment like satellite phones, night vision devices, bullet proof jackets and tactics of guerrilla warfare. The world must make sure that the freedom fighters have military efficiency.**

- **Terrain.** The terrain in most areas of southern Tibet, Kham and Amdo regions are mountainous with deep gorges and streams. **The region is sparsely populated and road communications vulnerable to disruption by weather and actions of freedom fighters. The terrain thus favours the freedom fighters.**

- **External Support.** Support by the US, EU and India is most important for successful liberation of Tibet. Without money, supply of weapons and other support, logistic support, safe sanctuaries, the movement cannot succeed. **External support has to be provided clandestinely. Political support and publicity to successful operations must be openly provided.**

Special Frontier Force

The Special Frontier Force (SFF), a secret Indian Army unit operating under the Research and Analysis Wing (RAW), can be considered to be the successor of Chushi Gangdruk Army. The need for a Tibetan guerrilla outfit for intelligence, surveillance and other clandestine activities was felt by multiple quarters in India. After the Chinese attacks in October 1962, the feasibility of raising a force comprising Tibetans to attack Chinese army from within Tibet was examined. A force, the SFF was raised under Brigadier Sujan Singh Uban (later Major General SS Uban) as the first commander of this force. The SFF commander is an army officer of Major General rank and is referred to as Inspector General, SFF. The director of Intelligence Bureau, Bhola Nath Mullick was also involved. He approached Dalai Lama's brother Gyalo Thondup, who was staying in Calcutta, to help in recruiting Tibetans to this guerrilla force from various Tibetan refugee camps in India. This force was to be used for intelligence gathering and clandestine operations in Tibet in case of any future Indo-China war. This arrangement led to the birth of SFF. Later the SFF was placed under RAW. This was the start of India's tryst with Tibetans, recruited and trained as an elite special operations force, for fighting a common enemy. As time went by, both the size and scope of this outfit increased. There are only a few recorded instances of SFF being used against China along the Indo-Tibet border. Various SFF units were placed from Ladakh to Arunachal Pradesh for intelligence gathering and surveillance. In 1971, SFF troops were involved in the Bangladesh Liberation War. Infiltrating into East Pakistan from the border town of Demagiri in Mizoram, SFF conducted guerrilla raids against Pakistani troops in Chittagong Hill Tract (CHT) region, codenamed 'Operation Eagle'. This action blocked the escape route of Pakistan Army's Chittagong-based 97th (I) Infantry Brigade. About 3,000 SFF troops took part in Operation Eagle, suffering a loss of 56 men; another 190 were wounded. The Centre had announced cash awards to 580 personnel. **Recently, SFF personnel, comprising of Tibetan soldiers led by Indian officers, played a key role in capturing important peaks on South Bank of Pangong TSO between August 29 and 31, 1921.** These indomitable Tibetan soldiers are carrying forward a legacy that began shortly after the Indo-China war of 1962. **Tibetan volunteers from the SFF could form the hard core of the Tibetan Liberation Army and provide leadership and trainers for the force.**

Geographical and Regional Consideration in Tibet

Tibet can be broadly divided into four regions. **North-Western Tibet** region is known as the "Lakes Region." The area is snow bound for most of the year. There is hardly any vegetation. This vast area is sparsely populated as there is shortage of potable water. Most of the lakes have salty water. Pangon Tso is the largest lake in the region. This region is highly militarized and is the area of confrontation between Indian and Chinese forces in recent years. It borders the Aksai Chin Region. The Lasha-Khasgar Highway G 207 passes through this area. The area is not suitable for operations of the Tibetan Liberation Army.

Southern Tibet region is most important for the security of India as it extends along Tibet's southern border from Demchok in Ladakh to Anini in Arunachal. The Tibetanung-Zambo (Bramhaputra) River originates near Mount Kailash and flows east across Tibet for 2400 km and enters India near Anini in Arunachal Pradesh. Indus River originates nears Mansarobar Lake and flows into India near Demchok in Ladakh. Langchankhambab (Sutlej River) originates near Mt. Kailash. The region lies between the Gangdise Mountain Range running east west along south bank of Bramhaputra River and the Himalayan range stretching from Ladakh to Arunachal. The area is well served by road network. It is well populated along the road network and contains a number of cities, towns and villages. However, there are also areas on the slopes of Mount Kailash, Nanda Devi Mountain opposite Himachal Pradesh and Uttarakhand, Kanchenjunga in Sikkim and Anini in Arunachal Pradesh which are extremely difficult terrain with few roads and villages. The area is ideal for establishment of bases by the Tibetan Liberation Army. This area is priority one for liberation. The Yadong County, lying between Bhutan and Sikkim is the most vital for security of the Siliguri Corridor and must be the first area to be liberated. Southern Tibet also includes the Kham region which extends from Mustang, north of Nepal to Anini.

Northers Tibet area is the area north of Lasha. The main road and rail communications from China to Tibet passes through this area. This region is too far from Indian borders for any assistance to be provided to the Tibetan Liberation Army.

Campaign Season for regular army is May to November in West Tibet, May to June and October to November in Eastern and Southern Tibet. July to September is monsoon season. **The best season for the Tibetan Liberation Army to operate is Nov to March or the winter. Most areas of Tibet get snow bound in winter. The temperature is sub-zero. Chinese**

Troops will be confined in their bases leaving the countryside under control of the Tibetan Liberation Army.

Benefits of Liberating Tibet

The benefits to India from liberating Tibet are:

- The border problem with China will be over once for all and considerable savings in defence expenditure will follow. The threat to Siliguri Corridor through Dokalam will be eliminated.
- Nepal will be cut off from China and Nepal's belligerence and anti-India stance will be over. Nepal will become fully dependant on India.
- China-Pakistan Economic Corridor will be closed and Pakistan will be isolated.
- China has been providing military and financial aid terrorist organizations of the North East since 1952. Chairman of ULFA has been given asylum by China. They need to be paid back in the same coin.
- With China in decline, India will be the Number 2 power in the world.

The benefits to the world from liberating Tibet are:

- Liberation of Tibet will certainly end the aggressive Xi Jinping Regime and usher in a more accommodative and friendly regime.
- The Arms race between China and its neighbours and the US will end and free up billions of dollars needed for fighting climate change.

Organizations Which Support Tibetan Independence

Organisations which support the Tibetan independence movement include:

- **Tibetan Youth Congress.** This organization is located at Dharmshala, the seat of the CTA. It claims 30,000 members. It could try to start the armed struggle and provide fighters.
- **International Tibet Independence Movement.** This organization is located in the State of Indiana in the US. It was formed in March 1995. It seems to be best placed to co-ordinate the armed freedom struggle. Could be useful in raising money and for propaganda.
- **International Tibetan Aid Organization.** It is located in Netherland. This organization was formed in 2004. It could perform similar activities in EU.

CIA supported Tibetan resistance with military and economic aid till 1973. They may chip in again under the Biden Presidency. **India has so far not supported Tibetan Independence or an armed freedom struggle in Tibet. But in view of Chinese belligerence in Ladakh, Dokalam and Arunachal borders, it may provide clandestine support to an armed freedom struggle in Tibet.**

Actions Required if CTA Agrees to Armed Freedom Struggle

In any conflict, surprise is key to success. Mao Ze Dong has himself written, "In guerrilla war, select the tactics of seeming to come from the east and attack from the west; avoid the solid, attack the hollow; attack, withdraw, seek a lightning decision." **If CTA wants an armed struggle to force the Chinese to concede independence or political and religious autonomy, they have to identify a leader to lead the struggle and get him to contact CIA and Indian intelligence to do the planning, recruiting, training, equipping and induction of these freedom fighters into Tibet.** Satellite phones should be used for communication and drones could be used to supply weapons, ammunitions, medicines. **The CTA and India could deny any involvement and blame the attacks on non-state actors.**

When to Start

There is strong resentment in the UN and many countries against the Chinese human rights violation in Xinjiang, Hong Kong and Tibet and its belligerence in South China Sea. All these countries will support liberation of Tibet and recognition of Taiwan in their own way.

China is facing many severe domestic problems. The unprecedented floods in July have severely damaged many cities and industries along the Yangtze and other major rivers. There is acute shortage of food. Stoppage of supply of certain key inputs like "chips" is hurting its electronic industry. The economic slowdown caused by the COVID 19 pandemic all around the world has slowed the demand for Chinese goods. This is causing severe unemployment problems among young Chinese.

Last but not least is that the Chinese Army is all bluster and no bite. China has lethal fire-power and nuclear capability. However, these are not battle winning advantage in asymmetrical warfare as we have seen in Vietnam and Afghanistan. In both cases the mighty US could not win. **The PLA soldiers in the field, all only sons with no battle experience, reluctantly forced to deploy to fight a determined enemy in a foreign land in hostile weather conditions have no appetite for war. They will bolt or surrender when things go badly.**

Action Plan

Preparatory Phase (December 2022 to December 2023)

- **Prepare an outline plan.** The aim should be to raise 9 battalions of SFF/Tibetan Liberation Army. These should be formed into three brigades. One brigade should be deployed in Ladakh, Himachal and Uttarakhand for operations across the border. One brigades should be deployed in North Sikkim for operations across the border. One Brigade in Arunachal for operations in Kham and Amdo regions. These brigades will function under Indian Army Formations till they can be deployed in liberated areas. These troops should be trained and equipped for winter warfare in the US and Finland. They should be trained in guerrilla warfare by the SFF. They should be provided artillery support by Indian army wherever possible from Indian territory.
- **Discuss participation of US and QUAD members in the project.** Their financial and military aid and intelligence inputs including satellite imagery are most important for the Tibetan Liberation Army. It will be difficult for India to bear the entire cost.
- Recruit, equip and train the force. Maintain maximum secrecy.

War of Liberation (December 2023 till objectives are achieved)

This will include the following:

- **Occupy Chinese defensive positions along the border which may have been vacated for the winter.** Attack Chinese troops when they come to occupy the defences and cause casualties.
- **Establish operational bases on defendable features within 30 km of the LAC.** These bases should be capable of being provided artillery support by Indian guns. These bases should be stocked with weapons and ammunition, rations and medical equipment and medicines and used for carrying out raids deep into enemy territory.
- **Carry out raids on Chinese settlers, their logistic bases, road construction and snow clearing units** with the aim of destroying maximum plant and machinery like earth moving and snow clearing equipment. This activity should start in February.
- **Destroy bridges and create landslides to block roads** likely to be used by Chinese troops to bring reinforcements and supplies. This activity should start in March.

- Capture isolated Chinese Border Guards Units and take over their weapons, accommodation and rations. Also attack Air Defence Units and destroy radars.
- Ambush supply convoys.
- Cause casualties and demoralize the Chinese troops.

Chinese infantry is reluctant to fight. Its morale is low. Now is the best time to establish domination over it. **China is an occupying power in Tibet. Tibetan Liberation Army can certainly count on support from the Tibetans themselves, India and the Western World.**

Summary

The official position of the CTA is to follow the Middle Way Path or to negotiate with China for grant of political, religious and cultural autonomy. **This path was proposed by Dalai Lama in 1987. China has not conceded any autonomy in the 35 years that has elapsed since. It is unlikely that it will concede any autonomy unless it is forced to do so by an armed or non-violent freedom struggle.**

Though armed freedom struggle ended in 1973 when the CIA stopped aiding the struggle, **protests and self-immolations continue inside Tibet indicating that many inside Tibet want freedom or at least self-rule.** The appetite for armed freedom struggle among Tibetans in exile is not clear.

The terrain in Tibet favours guerrilla warfare.

India and the free world have much to gain from a weakened China.

The fighting capability of Chinese infantry and armour is untested in battle. They being three year contract soldiers and only sons are unlikely to have any appetite for fighting.

SFF could be a source for Tibetan Freedom Fighters and Military leaders and Trainers.

Analysis

There are Tibetans in Tibet who are ready to lay down their lives while fighting for freedom. They have no access to military hardware and training. They also need military commanders who can plan and carryout guerrilla warfare. India and the world, particularly CIA and RAW need to get involved.

The CTA can publicly disown the freedom fighters and continue negotiations for the Middle Way solution.

Epilogue

There are over six million Tibetans who live in Tibet under Chinese colonial rule. They have no human rights. Their lands and businesses are handed over to Han and Hui Chinese settlers. Their women are forcibly married off to Chinese settlers. Their religion and cultural heritage are being systematically destroyed. Without outside assistance, all they can do is to self-immolate. Does India and the world care? Do the Tibetans in exile care?

There are about 150,000 Tibetans in exile. Most of them live in comfort in India, the US or EU. How many of them really care about what happens to about 6 million of their people who live as second-class citizen in their own country. India could produce great freedom fighters from the well-heeled upper crust. Mahatma Gandhi was a barrister. He gave up his suit and his lucrative profession and led India's non-violent freedom struggle in a "Dhoti". Netaji Subhash Chandra Bose came from a renowned upper crust family of Bengal. He gave up his career in the Imperial Civil Service and became a freedom fighter who led India's armed freedom struggle.Can Tibetans living in Tibet or in exile produce leaders like Mahatma Gandhi or Subhash Chandra Bose?

India and other world powers cannot attack China and liberate Tibet. Tibetans must fight for their freedom as the Taliban did in Afghanistan. India and the world must help them by providing them all the assistance they need. Tibetans inside and outside Tibet must find a way to take up arms and fight for their freedom.

The clash between the Chinese and Indian armies at Galwan in June 2021 amid the stand-off at the LAC in Ladakh has brought into focus the Chinese threat. The author feels that Indian and world political leaders have over-estimated and continue to over-estimate Chinese military capabilities and needs to adopt offensive defence as their core policy in dealing with China.

Present-day Indian rulers believe in preparing to defend our territory but not dominating the enemy and defeating them. When Mohammad Ghori used to attack the Somnath Temple of Gujrat, thousands of Indian volunteers (brave patriots with little training or military leadership) rushed to battle with whatever weapons they could muster and were massacred by Mohammad's well trained and well-equipped forces. The invaders went away with gold, jewellery and women. They kept returning year after year and sacked the Somnath Temple no less than thirteen times without effective resistance. **Things have not changed.We have fought four wars with Pakistan and won one in 1971. That victory was possible because Indira Gandhi was not afraid of going on the offensive. She had obtained necessary weapon systems from the Soviet Union and the armed forces were fully combat ready and motivated.** We ran out of ammunition for Bofors guns and coffins during the Kargil war and had to resort to emergency purchases. Politicians, people, men and media eulogize the sacrifices of the armed forces when a war or terrorist strike causes casualties. **Then everyone forgets the lessons of the war.** It is business as usual. **The economist and private sector keep rooting for more imports from China.** The armed forces and their requirements for modernization and maintenance are put on the back burner. Manpower is kept below strength to save money. **Regular intake of soldiers has been replaced by inducting soldiers on four-year contract.** Budget allocation for modernization remains unspent every year due to bureaucratic bungling. No one cares.

India and the world must assist any armed struggle Tibetans may take up to gain independence or real political and religious autonomy.

Bibliography

Chapter 1: History of Tibet

www. en.wikipedia.org

"UK Recognizes China's Direct Rule over Tibet" By Richard Spencer, The Daily Telegraph 5 November 2008

Chapter 2 : India's Relations with China

www. en.wikipedia.org

"India and China Row Over Border" BBC News, 14-11-2006.

Chapter 3: China's National Objectives

www. en.wikipedia.org

U.S. Department of Defence, "Military Power of the People's Republic of China 2007"

Congressional Research Service, "China Naval Modernization: Implications for U.S. Navy Capabilities"

Centre for Strategic and International Studies

www . global security.org/china

www. about.com/asian history

Chapter 4 : China Relations with Pakistan

www. en.wikipedia.org

"New Developments in Pakistan-China Relations" by Tanvir Ahmad Khan, Arab News August 6th, 2007

"Pakistan-China Defence Cooperation" by Dr Swaran Singh May 1996

"China-Pakistan-Myanmar: The triangular relationship needs careful watch" by C. S. Kuppuswamy

"Chinese Military Supplies to Pakistan" News behind the News, January 14, 2002

"China-Pakistan: An unholy nuclear alliance" by Siddharth Ramana, December 4, 2008

Chapter 5: China's Relations with Bangladesh

www. en.wikipedia.org

www. earthtimes.com

www. anglefire.com

www. southasianalysis.org

www. banglapedia.search.com

www.virtualbangladesh.com

Chapter 6: China's Relations with Shri Lanka

www. Wikipedia.org – Sri Lankan Army

www. en.wikipedia.org

www. Tamilnation.org

Chapter 7: China's Relations with Burma

www southasianalysis/paper5

www. en.wikipedia.org

Chapter 8: China' Relations with Nepal

www. en.wikipedia.org

www. Fmprc.gov.cn

www. China.org.cn

www. Country-data.com

Chapter 9: China's Build up in Tibet

www. en.wikipedia.org

www. Amnestyusa.org

www. Indiadefensereview.com

www. Shadowforeignpolicy.com

www. Globalsecurity.org

Chapter 10: Understanding Chinese Armed Forces

www. en.wikipedia.org

www. globalsecurity.org

www. bharatrakshak.com/landforces/army/1962war

Chapter 11: Helping Tibetans Liberate

en.wikipedia.org

Epilogue

About The Author

Col (Retd) Bhaskar Sarkar VSM was born in 1940. He graduated in civil engineering from Kolkata University in 1963. He joined IMA in April 1963 and was commissioned into the Corps of Engineers. **A graduate from Defence Services Staff College, Wellington, he served as Brigade Major of a Mountain Brigade in Nagaland, Second in Command of Armoured Division's Engineer Regiment, Commanding Officer of an Engineer Regiment, Chief Engineers of a Border Roads Project and in many staff appointments. He did management course at College of Defence Management in Secundrabad. He had three tenures in College of Military Engineering where he taught tactics and was also Head of Training. He has been decorated twice for distinguished service; VSM as commanding officer and COAS Commendation Card as Col Q, HQ Eastern Command.** He hung his boots after 28 years of distinguished service in the rank of Colonel. After retirement Col Sarkar joined the construction industry as a civil engineer and management consultant and served on many interesting projects. He was keen sportsman and his hobbies include wild life, gardening, travelling and charity work. A versatile writer, has over a hundred articles published in Journals like the Infantry, The Sapper and Merinews,com. He has fifteen published books in print and another 12 "e" books.

Books by the Author are Pakistan Seeks Revenge and God Saves. India, Tackling Insurgency and Terrorism; Kargil War, Past Present and Future, Outstanding Victories of the Indian Army, Thirty-nine Steps to Happiness, Practical Approach to Vaastu Shastra, Earthquakes, All we need to know about them, Nationalism: Economic Strategy for Survival of Developing Countries, An Introduction to Religions of the World, Who is Afraid of the Chinese Dragon? I am, Tackling the Maoist Menace. Bhaskar Sarkar's Author Profile on Smashwords is: http://www.smashwords.com/profile/view/Bhaskarsarkar1940 .